DARK SACRIFICES

DARK SACRIFICES
Copyright © 2022 by Allison Aldridge

All rights reserved. No part of this publication may be used or reproduced in any manner whatsoever without written permission except in the case of brief quotations embodied in critical articles or reviews.

This book is a work of fiction. Names, characters, businesses, organizations, places, events and incidents either are the product of the author's imagination or are used fictitiously. Any resemblance to actual persons, living or dead, events, or locales is entirely coincidental.

Cover design by Designer © 2022 by Damonza
Under Cover Design by © 2022 by Maja K.
Edited by Rare Bird Editing
Proofread by Kvonbehren
ISBN: 978-1-7332687-4-5

Second Edition : 2023

10 9 8 7 6 5 4 3 2

DARK SACRIFICES

ALLISON ALDRIDGE

ALSO BY ALLISON ALDRIDGE

Dark Radiance Series:
Dark Radiance (Book One)
Dark Sacrifices (Book Two)

FOR STEPHANIE WRIGHT,
THE WOMAN WHO INTRODUCED
ME TO THE WORLD OF STORIES AND
MADE MAGIC HAPPEN WHEREVER
SHE WENT.

Contents
THE SINNERS' WALTZ

Prologue	1
Chapter One	5
Chapter Two	12
Chapter Three	22
Chapter Four	37
Chapter Five	48
Chapter Six	61
Chapter Seven	74
Chapter Eight	85
Chapter Nine	97
Chapter Ten	108
Chapter Eleven	114
Chapter Twelve	122
Chapter Thirteen	136
Chapter Fourteen	141
Chapter Fifteen	150
Chapter Sixteen	156
Chapter Seventeen	159
Chapter Eighteen	165
Chapter Nineteen	169
Chapter Twenty	177
Chapter Twenty-One	186
Chapter Twenty-Two	198
Epilogue	202

Contents
THE REAPERS SYMPHONY

Chapter One	212
Chapter Two	219
Chapter Three	233
Chapter Four	245
Chapter Five	260
Chapter Six	269
Chapter Seven	278
Chapter Eight	290
Chapter Nine	298
Chapter Ten	302
Chapter Eleven	311
Chapter Twelve	317
Chapter Thirteen	323
Chapter Fourteen	334
Chapter Fifteen	340
Chapter Sixteen	346
Chapter Seventeen	355
Epilogue	362

SIGN UP FOR THE MONTHLY NEWSLETTER

TO RECEIVE SPECIAL OFFERS, GIVEAWAYS, DISCOUNTS, BONUS CONTENT, UPDATES FROM THE AUTHOR, INFO ON UPCOMING RELEASES, AND OTHER GREAT READS!

WWW.ALLISONALDRIDGE.COM

PLAYLIST

FIND THE FULL PLAYLIST & MORE ON SPOTIFY:
AUTHORALLISONALDRIDGE

LOSING MY RELIGION

THE RETICENT

DEEP END

HOLLY HUMBERSTONE.

MAKE IT TO ME

SAM SMITH

THE ENEMY

ANDREW BELLE

MONSTER

WILLYECHO

HORNS

BRYCE FOX

WRONG DIRECTION

HAILEE STEINFELD

FALSE GOD

TAYLOR SWIFT

11 MINUTES

YUNGBLUD, HALSEY, TRAVIS BARKER

Aspyn Faye
&
Finley Blackbourne

The Sinners' Waltz

A hell of her own making burned brighter than an angel could ever contain.

PROLOGUE
Aspyn Faye

Darkness wrapped its strong hands around my throat, pulling me deeper into the endless void. A sharp pain shot through my entire body, overtaking my thoughts as the heavy fog clouding my mind began to fade. Slowly I peeled open my eyes, lids heavy from sleep. Florescent spots floated across my vision like the tiny dancers I had once witnessed in a ballet performance. They spun in perfect unison, giving off a glimmer of repetition until the dancers took their final bows and flitted out of my eyes.

   I was in a dimly lit room with yellowing walls and just enough room for a bed and a single chair in the corner. A figure sat hunched over in the darkest corner they could find, but even through the shadows I could see the mess of black hair trying to mask my twin's sullen expression. Asher's head hung low — the heels of his hands driven into his eye sockets. There were deep purple bruises covering most of his face and leading underneath his dark T-shirt.

"Ash?" I called out in a pitiful whisper, my throat raw against the silent air as I tried to speak. My twin's head lifted, his eyes immediately snapping up to meet mine. Gasping slightly, I stared in shock at the vibrant green color which replaced the smoky shade that Asher and I had shared. I tried to place my elbows underneath me to sit up, but the fiery pain I felt in the darkness shot though my shoulder blades. Every attempt to sit only brought on a deeper burn. I felt sick, stomach turning over as a watercolor blur of images flashed across my vision. The blood — there was so much of it — mixed with ear shattering screams I could never unhear.

Asher stood and made his way over to me in a

way he only did when he was were trying to coax someone off the edge. My breathing came in short, shallow breaths as tears burned the corners of my eyes. The room around me became a smudged, mismatched vision of itself. I untangled myself from the sheets, which were twisted around me, and shot from the bed toward a connected bathroom. My legs buckled under me, and I caught myself on the lip of the bathroom counter.

"No, no, no," I whispered under my breath. Asher was in the doorway staring at me with a pitying look that I couldn't take at the moment. Spinning around clumsily, I slammed the door in his face and clicked the lock into place. The sound of his fists hitting the hardwood door reverberated off the tile floor. I rested my head against the surface, the blood pumping in my ears blocking out his pleas to be let in. My gut twisted as I reached back, placing a single hand near my spine to feel the damage before looking at it.

The damned were rarely spoken of when I was young; truly, they were just legends to keep us in line. But time and time again the nightmare had become a reality in the sleepy town of Idelwood. I turned slowly, taking in the girl staring back at me in the mirror. Black soot was spotted across my skin in random patches, and a matching set of deep purple circles hung underneath my eyes. Slowly I turned my back toward the mirror and craned my neck to see the damage. A hiss slid between my teeth as I caught sight of the deep cuts rounding out my shoulder blades. The black shirt I had been wearing hung in limp fabric pieces, and dried blood coated my skin in heavy drips.

My knees hit the tiled floor, a strangled cry breaking through my lips as I went. Splintered wood flew around me as Asher broke through the door. I leaned into the floor, my hands catching my body weight and refusing Asher's comfort.

This was the beginning of the end. I had danced on the edge of hell in a ballroom full of angels. But the dance was over now, and I had dropped the only lifeline which tethered me to the waltz. Leaving the boy with the brilliant red hair and sad smile alone in the middle of the swirling chaos, I threw myself full force into the inferno.

CHAPTER ONE
12 HOURS AFTER THE BALL

For as long as I could recall, it had always been three of us. The Faye twins and Finley Blackbourne. The redheaded boy who always laughed at my terrible jokes was also the voice of reason to Asher when he was determined to rebel against the council. He kept us from becoming one of the damned that haunted my nightmares, but in the end, you can only avoid your destiny so many times before it comes back to bite you in the ass.

Asher fell first. Or at least that is what I have been told, but from what I remember I threw myself into the fire not long after him. Not even the soft voice of reason could plead me off the edge.

Through hell and back.

A silent promise which hung around the three of us. Even the day everything went up in flames, we still clung to it. For me, I don't think I ever stopped believing in the words.

"How did we get here?" Finley's raspy voice broke through the thick silence. I shifted uncomfortably, as his presence made my skin buzz with joy. It was a feeling I had craved for so long that most days I thought it would drive me insane. Liliana Caldwell lay against a makeshift bed in the corner of the room. She was pretty banged up from her adventure through the woods, making her paler than the sheets which laid underneath her.

Mallory was dead, Delaney was somewhere planning Rowen's demise, and Tabitha was writhing in pain as the shock of all she had lost settled around her. I hadn't seen Gabe's face since he turned away from me, but I knew the mention of Claire Halloway was a painful one. Rowen's depiction of the girl's demise must be torturing him.

Rowen was alive. The fact circled around my mind in a violent dance. It gave me a headache right between my eyes. My gaze fell upon the girl who is the spitting image of her mother and unknowingly started a revolution. I couldn't help but envy her slumber. I kept my eyes locked on Liliana, trying my best to avoid the pull to look into the glare of the one person I managed to avoid since the day I fell. His hot gaze likes the fires from hell burned into my side.

"You know how we got here, Finley," I said, my whisper barely audible. Those were the only words I could manage to push through my lips—anything else would break open the wall I had worked so hard to build against him. With Asher missing in action and the boy I had distanced myself from just inches away from me, my whole being was on edge.

Finley always set my senses into overdrive when he was around. Every touch, look, and word which had been spoken in the past hours had been electrified by the years of distance. I felt like I couldn't piece two coherent thoughts together with him in the same room as me.

"I know the answer you want me to know. The one you have driven into my mind for practically two decades now, but not the truth, Aspyn," His husky voice was right next to my ear, sending shivers down my spine. I froze, watching as Lily's chest moved up and down in perfect rhythm. The room was silent for a while, Finley's and my breathing finding each other's patterns just as they were supposed to. "You don't have a real answer for me, do you?"

Whipping around, my nose brushed up against his. I glared up into his blue eyes. "Of course, I do. I broke my own heart to ensure you were untouched by those who wanted nothing more than to destroy you. Every decision I made was to keep you safe."

My back slammed into the wall. Finley's looming figure hovered above me. His arms hung loosely on either side of my head. I couldn't help but take in every line that had formed on his face. The years we had been apart had hardened him.

"You didn't need to protect me, Aspyn." Finley's hot breath brushed up against my face. The hairs on the back of my neck rose, and I fought the urge to squirm under his gaze. I couldn't give him the satisfaction of knowing he still got under my skin.

"Maybe not. But you would have followed after us, and the shame would have destroyed you in the end. I couldn't let us ruin you," I said through clenched teeth. "I wasn't going to be the one to rip out everything good in you for my own selfish pleasure."

"That wasn't your choice to make, Asp," Finley spoke softly, his voice almost silent.

"But it was the one I made and one I would make again. There is nothing either of us can do about it now." My voice shook with emotion as I finally allowed myself to get lost in his icy eyes. Finley held my stare for a moment before pushing himself off the wall he had trapped me against and began to walk out of the room.

My hand shot out, grasping his wrist. "Through hell and back."

"What?" Finley kept his back toward me. His entire body began to tremble as he fought the urge to close the distance between us. We both felt the tension pulse through our veins begging us to give in.

"Through hell and back—it was what we would say to each other when one of us was going to make a stupid decision." I smiled softly at the distant memories.

"You mean when Asher and you were going to do something stupid." I could practically see the smirk forming as he spoke.

"I went through hell and back to make sure you didn't fall with us. You would have never survived it. I almost didn't. Not when you had so much potential with the Elite. I mean, look at what you've accomplished — you're the one they go to when they need information. No matter how much I hate the council, I would have never taken that away from you. It was what you always dreamed of, Fin." My voice wavered as emotions crashed through me.

Finley turned to look at me, the wheels turning behind his eyes. "What I always wanted was to have you by my side, just like it was destined to be. Not to be Abel's errand boy."

"I hope that's what you still want at the end of all of this," I whispered. My heartbeat pounded against my ribcage, sending a sharp pain through me with each thud.

"It's not that simple, Aspyn. You can't just bat your eyelashes at me and expect everything to go back to how it once was." Finley's voice was angry. He let out a frustrated sigh, using his free hand to run his fingers through his hair.

I blinked back the tears that threatened to spill over my eyes. "Then why come back? Why did you bring Lil back to us when you could have been the good little errand boy you are?"

"I don't know anymore." His voice was tight, but his eyes gave away all his secrets. Fiery rage coated every section of blue it could find.

"Well, you better figure it out before Ash returns to us." I released my grip on his wrist and turned back to look toward the sleeping girl. "And if I was you, I would leave this room before he finds out you were anywhere near Liliana."

"As you wish, Aspyn." There were no emotions behind the words. My heart sank at the sound of the door clicking shut.

Chapter Two
Before

Dark-purple silk glistened against the pale white light that filled the strange room I stood within. My hands ran down the front of the dress, a simple thing with capped sleeves and a skirt that reached the floor in a pool of color. There were no embellishments on the fabric. The council wanted to keep everything plain and simple when it came to the Iunctura ceremony. They wanted the distractions to be kept to a minimum as we looked into the eyes of our future.

I stared directly into the mirrored wall. My light green eyes were smoky with frustration. They began to shine in the corners, making the thin, dark liner I had painted on my eyes smudge next the bridge of my nose.

This was my duty to honor traditions which had been set in stone since the creation, but it didn't make me want to be a part of the ritual. It was giving my entire life to the Elite Council's ideals, the same principles that cast Alexander Caldwell out months ago.

"You look lovely, sister." Asher's voice pulled me from my thoughts. He stood in the doorway watching me intently with the same eyes that stared back at him. My hands hung low, pulling against one another as I tried to contain my nerves in their grasp. Asher's brows pulled together at the sight. "Aspyn, we have discussed this."

I held my hand up, silencing his speech. "I know. The fact remains that it doesn't make it any easier."

"Even if the pair of you are not meant to be, it doesn't mean he will combust into flames. He'll still be around." Asher stepped into the room, keeping a distance between the two of us. I knew he felt the anger radiating off my skin as it began to hum. Turning on my heel, I faced my twin, both of our green eyes burning with an intense emotion I couldn't place. Asher narrowed his gaze at me. "I know that since Xander fell you've had a strong opinion about the way the Elites operate, but promise me you are not thinking about doing something stupid tonight."

I scoffed. "Of course not. I would rather die than lose my wings to those monsters."

"Watch your tongue—we wouldn't want the wrong person to hear those vulgar words of yours." A deep voice broke the tension in the air. One that I would know in every lifetime. Finley stood watching with amusement, his famous smirk plastered against pale skin. Both boys in the room were dressed in formal suits with the Elite's golden ornament pinned against the left lapel. It was a large hollow circle with a pair of wings connecting the piece. A sign to all who the wearer reported to in this gloomy small town.

Idelwood had been home for decades, and in that time the locals had begun to blend with our kind. None of them truly understood what they were walking among or who their sins were being reported to. Their minds were toyed with to overlook that the Elite never aged. Though most mortals were oblivious even before their minds were warped. Only the insanely stupid ones questioned anything that looked amiss. They were delt with swiftly and silently every time.

Smiling brightly toward the redhead, I reached up to play with my own ornament. It hung on a matching chain against my collar bone. "The only one eavesdropping is you, Fin."

"That is due to the fact that no one cares to listen to the Faye twins' constant bickering anymore." Finley chuckled as Asher shot him a glare. "Can I have a word with your sister?"

"Be my guest." Asher waved his hand toward me in annoyance before stalking from the room.

"Why must you push his buttons, Asp? You are going to drive him mad one day." Finley stepped through the door, setting the entire room on fire as he did.

I turned my back to him and eyed him through the mirror walls surrounding us. My voice shook as I spoke, "You shouldn't be in here."

"There are no rules that say I cannot wish my beautiful best friend good luck on the cusp of her Iunctura ceremony. You know I only have your best interest at heart." His voice was soft. Finley moved to close the distance between us as I screwed in the back of my earring. A rush of goose bumps trail across my exposed skin with his body standing so close to mine.

"The funny thing about that statement, though, is…" I turned around to face him. Finley's face so close I could feel the vibrations of my words brush up onto his lips. "The best interest of my heart always leads back to you."

A heavy breath caught in the back of Finley's throat as his eyes traveled down to meet my painted lips. I debated closing the gap between us. The act was treason, and the only rule of the Iunctura was a clear no physical contact with other potential mates. If we were caught in this position, we would become two of the damned.

"We can't," I whispered, but my voice failed to put any authority to the words. We both stilled, neither able to find the strength to pull away from the other.

Finley sighed, resting his forehead against mine. "I know."

My heartbeat quickened, thumping in an erratic rhythm against my ribcage. I tried to find Finley's, praying it was synchronized with mine just as the other half of my soul was. But I couldn't hear anything over my own heart's flutter as a warm flush started at the tips of my ears. Neither of us moved, as my body begged to lean in just an inch closer.

The hum of our skin wanted nothing more than to collide, lips hungry for the first taste of each other in what seemed like an eternity. In reality it had only been a few hours. The last moments of us tangled up with each other as the morning sun peeked between the mountaintops of Idelwood were ones I would store in my brain forever. The ceremony does not lie, and you cannot change the fact that the ceremony may reveal someone who your heart did not desire. No matter how much you begged and pleaded with it.

"Well, well, well, what do we have here? Some

troublemakers, I see."

I slammed my body against the mirrored wall as a new voice spoke. Each glass panel shook violently with the motion. Finley stood in the opposite corner of the room, trying to place the same amount of distance between the two of us as I had. My gaze trailed up to meet the blue eyes of Ravana Chadwick. She leaned lazily against the door frame. A single finger trailed up and down the wooden lining as she watched us with a murderous glint in her glare. Ravana wore a floor-length gown similar to mine, but hers was a stark white. Her burgundy hair stood out against it, making the woman look angelic in her devilish ways.

"Ravana." My voice cracked as I stared in horror at her. My eyes slowly left hers, traveling to meet Finley's oddly calm ones. "It's not what you think."

"Oh? I believe it is exactly what I think." Ravana's once simple smirk morphed into an inhuman grin, a silent threat of our impending doom filling the air. "I think you were breaking the one rule of the Iunctura ceremony. Well, I should say Aspyn was, as it is the twins' night, after all. Don't you realize there is no fraternizing with each other with only…"

Her pale talon peeled off the framework of the door to examine a non-existent watch around her wrist with a narrowed look. "Only ten minutes left to spare."

Finley advanced toward Ravana, standing tall against the dark evil which surrounded her. "You didn't see anything, Chadwick. Why don't you run off to entertain Abel? I am sure ten minutes is enough time for the both of you."

I sucked in a hiss. "Finley."

My warning didn't faze either of them as they continued to glare at each other. Ravana batted her eyes toward Fin, making sure to let the dark lashes brush up against her pale skin. In this light she almost appeared innocent. The look could have rivaled the innocent nature Mallory Manson portrayed to the world any day. Ravana leaned in slowly, placing one hand flat against Finley's chest before leaning into him. Her eyes glistened with mischief. "Would you like to find out?"

My face dropped, glowing red glazed over my vision, and I had the urge to rip that hand from her body as each nail scratched against Finley's dress shirt. Her fingers toyed with the buttons, begging them to fall open at her command. Ravana's eyes shot toward me smirking in triumph at my anger. I clamped my mouth shut, teeth grinding together as I tried not to scream at the woman in front of me. She had caught us. She had the power.

"This will just be our little secret, loves, but don't think I won't come to collect my payment one day." Ravana licked her lips, eyeing Finley like he was a prize ready for the taking. Before either of us could respond, she flicked her wrist against the white material billowing around her legs and sent it flying after her as she traveled down the hall.

Finley released a haggard breath, craning his neck over his shoulder to look back at me. "I should get to my place before we cause any more trouble for ourselves."

I bobbed my head down, looking toward the floor. He strolled over, laying a single kiss against my hairline before whispering, "Good luck, Asp."

Then he was gone. Leaving me to debate the ideals of the council once again.

Chapter Three
Before

The Iunctura was a ritual to join two souls together. Its purpose was to merge the souls back into one, as it had once been written in the heavens during the creation. Mortals twisted this sick tradition into what is now viewed as soulmates, but they had a choice in the matter. The ceremony was held for an entire week at the change of seasons.

Each day a set of two were chosen to be matched. All it took was a single drop of the participants' blood, and their entire life was displayed out on a silver platter for them.

As each ceremony ticked by the past week, the dread in my stomach bubbled up further. Asher and I had been told we would be participating in the Fall Assimilation. The only thought I'd had since then was the idea that Finley would not be my match. The ritual was just another stone on top of my already crumbling state. I had been reminded countless times that the ceremony was a good thing, and I should be grateful to be participating in such a coveted ritual. The idea made me sick.

Two nameless council members guided me down a vanilla-colored hallway. Dotted along the plain hall were dark wooden doors and behind them, rooms which matched the mirror-walled one I had just been held in. I hummed the light tune of the death march in my head, matching my feet hitting the tiled floor to the beat.

"That is a tad bit morbid, don't you think, sister?" Asher appeared, cutting in front of the man to my left to fall in step with me. I toyed with the simple gold band on my left finger; the same one adorned Asher's as well. The rings were meant to be a symbol of the ceremony. Abel, the head of the Elites, had handed a pair to each of us this morning. The metal would be branded with the name which appeared today, and a matching one would be handed to our "soulmate." It was a silent promise to the other, but I only viewed it as a reminder of the lack of choice I had in my life. Asher spoke softly for my ears only, "I know it doesn't matter much coming from me, Aspyn, but if I had to wager on two people made for each other, it would be the two of you."

A sad smile broke across my face. "It means everything to me coming from you, Ash."

We came to a standstill in front of two large blood-red doors, the intricate carvings etched into the surface swirled together in chaotic lines. If you stood back a few feet, the lines fell in place to create a pair of wings, and every so often if the light changed, they appeared to be fluttering against the shine of the door.

Both men slipped past us and through the doors before being replaced by the smiling face of Rowen Caldwell. Her story was tragic in it of itself, as the person she was destined to be with had been ripped from her life when he fell. I had never witnessed two people more fiercely in love than Xander Caldwell and Rowen. Xander had always had a rebellious streak in his nature — most claimed he was destined to fall — but somehow even that didn't make his fate any easier to swallow. But Rowen held her own against the Elites. It was comical to me that she was hiding the fact that the fallen rebel and perfect prodigy were still involved behind a glittering smile.

Rowen stood tall as she leaned against the wood. A long emerald-green dress with a beaded belt brought out the red in her strawberry hair. "It is a miracle you two aren't bickering."

"I'm too nervous to bicker with him," I mumbled. Asher's hand shot out, latching with mine for comfort. I squeezed it in return, staring straight into Rowen's soft eyes.

"You have nothing to worry about, Aspyn," Rowen said, one hand running down my arm as she tried to soothe my nerves. "Xander sends both of you his well wishes."

I dropped my eyes to the tiled floor, a sick feeling filling the pit of my already nervous stomach. "How is he?"

Rowen began to respond but the red doors flew open, causing her to choke back the incriminating words. She motioned us forward into the room. I stared straight ahead into the large round chamber. The entire space held wooden pews which stacked on top of each other like risers at the high school football field. They reached father into the never-ending glass ceiling than my naked eye could track. Abel was in the center of a slab of granite that stretched across the room with his eleven other minions on either side.

In the center of the room was a large basin filled with holy water. The liquid sloshed around the curved edges. The shine of the water glistened off the glass paneled ceiling where it would mirror the water's images during the ceremony. Light murmurs traveled around us as Asher and I walked up to our designated spot behind the water basin hand in hand. Rowen stepped just a few feet ahead of us to whisper in Abel's ear.

Shrill bells of a nursery rhyme silenced the chatter of the room. Abel stood, hands planted on the table's surface, his booming voice reverberating off the walls. "Welcome everyone to our final Iunctura ceremony of the season. As most of you have been made aware, the Faye twins have graciously accepted the opportunity to be matched earlier than their intended time."

His dark eyes glared in my direction at the comment. I resisted the urge to smirk in his direction knowing full well I had not accepted willingly. Even Asher's coaxing had been useless in those moments. It had taken Abel's threat of the removal of my wings to finally make me swallow my pride and agree to this charade. I returned his look with a hardened one of my own, challenging him to out me to every Elite angel in this room.

Abel blinked once before turning his attention back to the crowd. "Rowen Caldwell will be leading the ceremony tonight."

Rowen turned her head toward the man as she waited for his signal to begin. He only nodded in her direction before returning to his seat in a large metal chair he treated as if it was own personal throne.

I squeezed down hard on Asher's hand, bracing

myself against the sound of Rowen's heeled steps as she made her way to us. Turning my gaze away from Rowen, I looked up into the silent crowd of angels gathered to watch my downfall. Bright blue orbs stared back toward me as I caught sight of the familiar red head sitting just feet away. My breath caught in throat at the sight of his sad eyes. We would never be the same after today.

A featherlight touch on my shoulder startled me out of Finley's intense gaze. I looked up at Rowen's grim face. "You are up first, Aspyn."

In her hand she gripped the handle of the steel blade. The base was a deep mahogany which stabilized the knife from shaking underneath Rowen's tremors. I reached out for the knife, the cool wood almost slipping out of my sweaty palm. My feet carried me silently to the basin, each step vibrating the liquid with heavy tremors. With the blade pointed toward me, one misstep could coat the shimmering white marble floor with my blood.

Abel watched intently over his wire frame glasses, smirking at the pain he found hidden in my stare. Pulling my eyes upward, I found

Finley's watchful look. He simply nodded toward me. I raised my left hand over the holy water to ensure once I made the cut, no blood would stain the pristine marble underneath me.

The blade sliced down against the delicate skin of my palm, causing me to hiss out in pain. It was the only sound until the blood began to flow down into the water. It mixed with the liquid and turned it light pink, which smeared inside the surface as it began to gather together and swirl around the basin in a jerking motion. Then the water shot up toward the glass ceiling. I gasped, taking a step back to avoid being drenched against the roar of the water's wave.

A picture began to form within the liquid's surface, but all I could see was the watery reflection of Finley staring back at me from the other side of the swell. Finally, the water slammed back into the bowl, leaving a single name written on a rough piece of thick embossed paper in the middle of the bowl. Rowen dipped her hand into the liquid and pulled the soaking note closer to her face.

Rowen smirked before she spoke to all the eager

ears listening in the room, "The soul which reflects your own is Finley Blackbourne."

I wheezed out a sigh of relief, watching as the redhead moved from his spot to stand next to me. The pounding of my heart slowed but kept up its constant flutter that was always present when Finley was around. He arrived behind me moments later, one of his hands coming up to rest of the small of my back. Finley's hot breath tickled my ear as he spoke, "See, I told you it would be fine, Asp."

Rowen was wiping the blade clean with a dark cloth to ready it for my twin. I could only bob my head slightly in repose to Finley, the nerves of my brother's choosing still lingering in my stomach. Asher stood tall over the basin, no visible fear in his demeanor as he slit the inside of this left palm. He clenched his hand together and let the blood drip slowly into the bowl before stepping back just in time to avoid the wave spouting through the air. This time the water responded in a violent surge. The entire chamber shook, sending screams of terror rippling through the crowd. I stepped back into Finley who gathered me into a protective hold.

The water swung left, causing large pieces of a column to rain down toward the pair of us. A scream escaped my lips, and I tried to dart toward Asher, who had thrown his hands over his head to shield himself. Finley pulled me back as a sharp piece of stone flew in our direction. He threw his body over mine, blocking my view of the chaos. I could hear what sounded like thunder crashing as if a storm had begun in the holy water. This version of the liquid was one I had never seen before in my entire existence.

Then it was silent.

Lifting myself out of Finley's grip, I found myself staring at the destruction the water's wrath had scattered around the small chamber. The room was covered in a thin sheen of droplets and rubble, causing the other spectators of the ceremony to cower around one another.

Asher stood from his crouched position, where he had been when I lost sight of him, but now a matching piece of parchment of the one I had just received was stuck between his fingertips. Rowen made no move to see what was upon the paper. Her body trembled from the corner of the room she hid in, wide eyes watching as my brother said, "Liliana Caldwell."

Asher met Rowen's gaze. Terror settled in the angel's eyes before she bolted from the room. A loud bang rang out around us, making me snap my head in Abel's direction. The leader of the Elite was red with fury. "You must be mistaken, boy. Read it again."

"It only reads Liliana Caldwell, sir." Asher's voice was monotone as he spoke. The answer enraged Abel who responded by rounding the table and rubble to get to Asher. I stepped up toward my twin, reaching him the same time as Abel.

Abel reached down toward the thick paper and ripped it from Asher's bloodied hand. "The ceremony never lies. Whoever this Liliana is, I want her found. And the one who conspired this plan must be brought in front of the council immediately. The fact that she is hiding behind the surname of one of the damned is no coincidence."

"Yes sir," Asher mumbled, meeting my worried eyes.

"Everyone is dismissed." Abel threw the scrap of paper into Asher's chest before stalking toward the council.

I gripped Asher's bicep and pulled him through the crowd of terrified angels. Each one of them we passed flinched away from Ash as he brushed past them. Finley trailed close behind us, watching to ensure that no harm came to any of us.

We flooded out of the double doors and into the dimly lit hallway. I veered left into a room that matched one we had all stood in earlier that evening. The door slammed shut as soon as we all were fully in the room.

Asher began to pace back and forth in the small room, making the space feel claustrophobic. His intense eyes stared down at the stranger's name who shared the same last name of our closest friends.

"Did you see anything in the water, Ash? When

it first shot up, I saw Fin, but I just thought it was his reflection through the sheet of water." I stepped in front of him to block his path, but Asher only marched around me to continue his pacing.

"Yes, I saw a girl who looked almost identical to Rowen. At first, I thought it was her, but this girl—" Asher paused for a moment, running his hand through his hair. "This girl had eyes that match Xander's. They were the same blue as his son Nathaniel's. She was stepping off a bus, and her strawberry hair was blowing in the wind. This girl, Liliana, was the most beautiful creature I have ever laid eyes on."

The pain in Asher's voice wavered in and out, cutting through me like a knife. Finley moved forward, breaking the intense silence after a moment. "Asher, you know that it is not possible for this girl to look like both Row and Xander. He is fallen, and we all know what becomes of a child who is the product of both our bloodlines."

My shoulders drooped. Nothing about this situation made any sense, and now with the reality of the one person who completed my brother never coming into this world, I felt numb. A shockwave of regret pumped through my veins as I watched Asher's emotions show on his face.

Asher turned on his heel to face Finley's stare full on with his own agitated one. "I am aware, Finley, but why would she appear at the ceremony if the soul was never to be used?"

"It sounds like some type of sick joke being played on you," I whispered, looking up toward my brother. His face contorted in pain. What I wouldn't give up to take it all away or have the right answer. Stepping forward, I reached out to place my hand against his arm, but he pushed me away. Asher mumbled something inaudible before storming off toward the door. It swung open to reveal Mallory Manson. She stood in a plain floral gown which was now dripping wet from the monsoon.

"I wouldn't go out there if I were you." Mallory's voice was tight with anger she was trying to suppress. "The rumors are already beginning to swirl, and they think you were instructed to orchestrate that little stunt back there."

"Let me guess, they all believe Xander was pulling the strings behind the scenes, and Asher followed along because of his blind loyalty to him," I hissed at Mallory. The harshness in the words weren't directed at her but to the Elites' idiotic ideals which brainwashed their most devoted followers.

Mallory nodded once, her sharp eyes watching all of us like a hawk looking for its next prey. "It is bad this time. I don't think you two are going to be able to just sweep this one under the rug without some type of miracle."

Chapter Four
Before

Mallory's words came as no surprise. She was often the one in our tight knit group to acquire the latest gossip being spread across Idelwood before it even traveled through the wind to the next ears willing to listen. The girl blended in with her surroundings so well you would never know she was there until Mallory had struck. She was a deadly beautiful combination.

I hadn't seen Asher much since he had pushed past the Manson girl. My twin was most likely sulking over that ridiculous name scrawled out on the parchment. Mallory had gone on to explain that the council believe not only Asher was involved in this madness but me as well.

They suspected neither of us could pull off a stunt such as this without the other entangled with in it. The news of the incident had traveled back to Xander quickly, most likely by a very upset angel who had fled from the scene in hysterics.

Idelwood felt tense no matter where I stepped. Even my favorite booth in the back of Celia's café with a cup of freshly brewed coffee did nothing to untangle the nerves twisted up in me. My skin crawled with the thought of all eyes being trained on every move I made. Though one pair of bright eyes always stuck out in the swarm of angels crowding the cobblestone square.

Claire Halloway, the preacher's daughter, smiled brightly at me while waving one hand in my direction. She turned back to the conversation she was having with the stranger in front of her. The girl had taken quite a liking toward our misfit group, and I had to say she fit in quite nicely into the missing space. Almost as if it was meant to be hers. She knew nothing of what we truly were, which made her friendship all the more valuable. Claire had a genuine heart with a laugh that lit up an entire space she stood in.

Rowen had been pushing to divulge our secret to Claire for months now. I protested the idea adamantly—the Halloway girl gave us a sense of normalcy and she didn't deserve to be brought into this madness. Telling her about the creatures which had taken up residence in Idelwood long before she arrived on this earth would shatter that illusion.

I was pulled from my thoughts by a gentle squeeze upon my hand. Finley walked beside me, his hand grasped firmly in mine, through the fringed snow that covered the mountains just outside the borders of Idelwood. Xander had summoned a meeting with the group. He may have fallen, but that doesn't mean he ever stopped being the one who called the shots when things got bad. Though the stakes of this particular event had never been as high as they were now.

The meeting spot since his fall from grace was the same every time, a clearing that overlooked the mountain peaks, just far enough away from prying eyes. You could see the whole world, or at least everything for miles around when standing up here. Breaking through the familiar fog clinging to the ground, I caught Asher's eye as he spoke intently with Xander. Rowen was just off to the side listening carefully while Delaney and Mallory Manson conversed with each other in the trees lining the clearings edge.

Xander tracked Asher's sightline, turning over his shoulder to greet us. Dropping my hand from Fin's, I dashed toward Xander. My entire body collided with his as I threw myself into a much-needed hug.

"I've missed you," I sputtered out, the emotions of the Iunctura ceremony finally coming to the surface. It had been nearly a month since I had last seen Xander, and in moments after the ceremony I had needed him more than ever. Pulling back from the hug, I looked up at the taller man who had somehow managed to look older since the last time I had seen him. His mouth was set in a grim line, eyes pulled taut showing deep purple circles underneath them. "It is bad, isn't it?"

"It's not good, that's for sure," Asher said from

behind Xander, arms crossed against his chest. He looked just as tired as Xander did, making me wonder if Asher had been with the fallen angel since the second he left my sight days ago. I took a step back, meeting Finley's light touch as he placed his palm against my lower back.

The Manson sister had moved closer to the interaction, waiting for Xander to begin explaining who the girl Asher had seen could possibly be. But it was Rowen who broke the silence. "I'm pregnant."

My eyes bulged out of my skull as I looked toward the trembling angel. Her strawberry hair blew violently in the wind as she pulled the large peacoat she was swimming in around her petite from. The words stuck in the back of my throat as I continued to stare toward Rowen. Finley's hand curled into my back, his fingers absentmindedly digging into the leather jacket I wore.

"You're joking, right?" Delaney Manson said, venom coating her words.

"No, she is not, and I would watch the tone you take with her, Delaney." Xander's voice darkened toward the girl, causing Delaney to cower into herself. He had a way of making a simple threat feel worse than it was intended too ever be. I stepped away from Finley's grasp and placed a hand against Rowen's arm, waiting for Xander to continue, but he clenched his jaw shut, the bone popping in and out as he ground his teeth together.

"What are we going to do?" My voice was soft in the howling wind. I met Asher's stare, pleading for him to give us answers none of us had

"No one is to know of this until we are unable to conceal the situation anymore," Xander's rough voice said. "With the exception of Claire Halloway."

"What," I screeched, sending a few lingering crows flying up into the clear blue sky. Finley was at my side in an instant as I tried to advance on Xander. I knew the man with the newly vibrant eyes would never intentionally cause me any harm, but Finley was still wary of the fallen angel.

The power Xander had obtained when the council had stripped his wings was something none of us had ever seen. The redhead caught my upper arm, pulling me backward into him.

The corners of my eyes burned with hot angry tears as I glared toward Xander. "You aren't thinking about dragging that poor girl into this are you?"

Everyone halted in place, the stillness in both Asher and Xander answering the question fully. I groaned inwardly, throwing my head back in disgust. "You have got to be kidding me right now. Whatever is going on, we can handle it ourselves without bringing a mortal into the mess as well. Let's not forget the fact that she is the pastor of Idelwood's daughter. What happens when she goes and blabs to her father's entire congregation? We would all be stripped of our wings then. Is that what you want, Xander? For all of us to be damned just as you are?"

Xander's face contorted in pain at the mention of any of the group having the same fate he was handed. I opened my mouth to speak once more but Asher's voice cut me off, "That is enough, sister."

I turned my angry stare on him, meeting the

same intense blaze in his gaze. Simply rolling my eyes, I turned on my heel and began the walk toward the trail leading to the cars.

Rowen's hand shot out and caught my jacket's sleeve, freezing me in place. I glanced down at her grasp before meeting her pleading eyes. "Aspyn, we must tell Claire about what we are. If we don't, Nathaniel and this baby will have nowhere to flee when the time comes. You know what the council will do if they get the child in their grasp."

"You think the baby is going to survive? When has any other infant survived being the product of what we are and what Xander has become?" I whispered.

Rowen nodded, "Call it mother's intuition, but this child is going to be special. I feel it in my bones."

"Every mother believes that to be true, Row, but it doesn't change the facts of the situation." I ripped my arm away and raced down the snowy slope. Loud footsteps followed after me, which I assumed to be Finley's, but as I turned to meet his gaze, I was met with another. My twin's look blazed with a fury that I had never seen before.

"You know, I don't get you, Aspyn." Asher's harsh voice cut through the wind, "One moment you hate the council and are determined to destroy all they stand for and the next you refuse to be anywhere near the two people who have saved our asses more times than I can count. Xander and Rowen are trying to do what is best for all of us."

"You mean the baby, right Asher?" I laughed, throwing my hands up in the air before they landed on my hips, "What are they going to name her? Liliana? Oh, and let me guess — that is the girl who was prophesized to be your other half? Even if that were true, do you think that you would ever have a happy ending in the situation we're in? Once this child is born, alive or not, Abel will snuff it out just like he does with every problem the council comes upon. And don't think for a mere second that a mortal girl such as Claire Halloway will be capable of outsmarting them."

"You are selfish," Asher yelled toward me. His words bounced off the branches of the surrounding trees as I began to descend down the mountain.

"Better to be selfish than damned," I shouted back at him.

"You only look out for yourself and Finley. Now that someone else needs your help, you just throw them aside as if they meant nothing to you. Even your own blood can't get through that thick skull of yours to make you realize what is at stake here."

"I don't just look out for myself or Finley." I whipped around and slammed into his towering figure. He loomed over me, an angry heat radiating off his body. "I am constantly trying to ensure you don't do something stupid in the council's eyes or that Delaney isn't getting caught practicing that dark magic she had taken a liking to."

My hands shoved against his broad chest with every hateful word that spewed out of my mouth, but he stood planted in place. I froze glaring at the center of his black T-shirt. "So don't you dare make it seem like I have no regard for anyone else but myself. What is occurring is way bigger than some silly incantations or simple rule breaking, Asher. Even uttering the words is treason punishable by removal of one's wings. I will not stand by and watch you all destroy yourselves. Are you really willing to risk everything we have worked for to maybe save a soul who, if she does survive, could destroy us all?"

"If it was Finely, would you even question it?"

I did not have to respond to the question. We both already knew the answer.

Chapter Five
Before

Eight days. That is how long it had been since the secret of Xander and Rowen's child was revealed to us. I continued on with life, avoiding both Asher and Finley every time we almost came in contact with each other.

My brother could barely look me in the eye. I could still feel the intense anger he was harboring, and it was beginning to weigh heavy on me. I never wanted to choose sides. Me walking away was just that, but in Asher's eyes I had chosen the wrong one. Rowen didn't deserve to be punished by the council, but the consequences of keeping this secret in this town were fatal. Even if their ideals were nonsensical and cruel, we followed the council's ways like the good little soldiers we were trained to be. Finley especially.

He wanted to climb as high as he could in the council, and now Xander had threatened to take that hope away. The thought made me sick to my stomach. Neither of them deserved to be judged under such a tight microscope. None of us did.

I leaned back against the mismatched plush cushions that lay across the floor in the Crypts. Celia stood hunched over the long wooden table that took up the middle of the room, her nose shoved into the spine of a book. She was trying to find any case in which a child of both sides had survived. From the deep crease folding into her forehead, I could see she was having no such luck. Behind me, Mallory huffed loudly, shoving books into their respective places on the large bookshelves which surrounded us. Each leather-bound book slammed into place harder as anger grew through her tiny body.

Mallory had always been the soft one of the Manson triplets — or that was how she portrayed herself. Underneath the bubbly girl, Mal was the deadliest of the three, as her beauty was a facade to the trickster whose anger rivaled even Lucifer himself. You never knew which Mallory you were going to encounter on any given day. Today it seemed as I would receive the wrath of the girl as I felt her heated skin hum with rage. Each slammed book shook the lamp sitting on the end table next to me.

"Mallory doll, please be careful with those." Celia eyed the fuming girl with amusement. "Some of those are as old as you are, after all."

Mallory threw a glare over her shoulder at Cee, who only rolled her eyes at the girl. "Well, if you want it done a different way, why don't you ask princess over there? She seems to have some time on her perfectly manicured hands."

I scoffed at the comment. "We both know you're angry with me, which is why your insults hold no weight in my mind. Why don't we just get this over with? You can yell and scream at me all you want where no one's prying ears can listen in."

"I don't know what you are insinuating, Aspyn. Why would I be angry with you? It's your choice not to support your friends." Mal turned back toward the shelf and slammed down another hardcover, causing the wood to dip with the force of her blow.

"All right, girls, let's hash this out now." Celia moved around the table to stand in between where I sat, and Mallory stood. I rolled my eyes, licking my finger to flip the page of the book I had been pretending to read, but it disappeared from my grip. Celia smirked down toward my glare. "Stand up."

Dusting the lint from my black jeans, I stepped toward the fuming girl with some hesitation. "Mal, look, I am sorry, but this is my decision to make. I am sure Xander, and Rowen will be better off without me meddling in the mess they have gotten themselves in."

"It is the wrong decision, Aspyn." Mallory spun around to face me. Her words filled with passion. "This isn't some mess. This is a life we are talking about."

"A life that may never be lived, Mallory, but all of you neglect to remember that detail when we are speaking of this," I shot back, my fire-filled words sparring with hers in the silence. Celia stepped closer to us, ready to break apart a fight if Mallory's anger got the better of her.

"Then why would she appear in your own brother's ceremony? The ceremony does not lie; it wasn't a mistake. The girl was grown, and she was arriving back in Idelwood after being away for years. Do not tell me that doesn't mean anything to you."

"Of course it does, Mal. I want Asher to be happy but not at the cost of him or any of us becoming what Xander has become."

Mallory let out an angry breath. "You have always been so wrapped up in the idea of falling out of the heavens that you can't even see how much the council has warped your mind. No matter how much of a rebel you believe yourself to be, Aspyn, you could never truly devote yourself to anything other than those twelve men leading this cult."

Mallory's words came out in one long hiss before she slammed her shoulder into me and stormed from the room. Only the sound of the shifting bookshelves echoed through the chamber as Celia, and I watched where she had gone.

A long sigh escaped my lips as I ran one hand down my face. Turning to Celia, my voice pleaded for her advice, "What am I supposed to do now, Cee? Everyone hates me because I refuse to get involved in something that can only end badly for all of us."

"Unfortunately, that isn't something I can answer for you, doll." Celia cupped the side of my face, sending me a sad smile. "Though I think there is one person who is willing to hear you out no matter what has been said."

I shrugged out of her touch. "Why are you always right?"

"It's a part of my charm." Celia flashed me a smirk, turning to dive back into the book she had been reading. I groaned and launched myself down into the pillows.

The snow had begun to melt as spring sprouted around the mountain top, leaving a sloshy mix of dirt and ice behind. I shivered as a chilly breeze brushed underneath my worn leather jacket. Everything around the clouded mountain was drained of color, sending me instantly into a sullen mood as I waited for the other party to arrive.

A shrill ring sounded out, bouncing off the tree line and causing my heart to beat violently against my chest. I dug in the back pocket of my jeans for the cellphone and flipped open the blaring device. "Hello?"

My eyes wandered around the clearing's edge, waiting for a figure to emerge from their shadows, but nothing even swayed in the wind. Finley's raspy voice broke me from my fear-ridden thoughts. "Where are you? I thought I was going to meet you at Celia's."

"Shit," I mumbled, running one hand over my clammy face. "I'm sorry. I forgot with everything that's going on right now. Ash is still not speaking to me, and it's just making everything suck even more than it already does."

"I know." Finley's understanding words made the guilt forming in the pit of my stomach crawl up into my throat. "How about you meet me at our spot in an hour? I am sure I could cheer you up."

The soft crunch of a stick behind me revealed I was no longer alone on the mountain. I craned my neck to meet the intense gaze of Xander Caldwell. His inhumanly vibrant sea-blue eyes made me squirm as I composed myself enough to reply. "Yeah, that sounds great, Fin. I'll see you in an hour."

"Okay." Finley paused for a moment. "I love you, Asp."

Sucking in a shallow breath, my eyes still trained on Xander, I said, "I love you too. See you in a bit."

The line went dead, and the sinking feeling of guilt doubled. I was lying to Finley, and even if it was to keep him out of the line of fire, I didn't think he would see it the same way. Finley would be furious with me for taking this on alone, but it was for his own good that he stayed as far away from this mess as possible.

"Thank you for meeting me," I croaked out to the fallen angel. Xander nodded once, still waiting for me to crack under his knowing gaze. Even I knew that he wasn't truly angry with me, only disappointed in my actions, which I had to admit were out of line.

I opened my mouth to speak, but nothing came out, making me close it immediately and glare at the dirt covered snow below me.

"I know." His voice broke through the silence. My eyes shot up to him as he continued, "I know you are sorry. The fact that we are standing here right now proves that much to me. We all know you, Asp. You take your anger out on the ones you love when you're scared of them being harmed."

"I am sorry for that as well." I looked away from him, ashamed of my own actions. "You're wrong though; I'm not scared for myself. I am petrified at the idea of anything happening to Asher or Finley, and the thought of mixing the Halloway girl in this world makes matters even worse. She doesn't deserve to have the council's wrath rained down upon her if they find out what she's hiding."

"Every brewing war has casualties. Claire understands this, and she agreed to help." Xander stepped forward to close the distance between us. "She took the news better than any of us expected when Rowen explained everything to her. We all were expecting more of an outburst, but it was as if she had already figured it out for herself. She came around only a few days later with an agreement to help."

"I hadn't realized you were going to tell her so soon," I said, my voice quiet in the soft breeze. Biting down on my bottom lip, I treaded lightly on my next words. "You know my decision has nothing to do with me not loving you and Row like family, right?"

"Aspyn, if that were entirely true, your decision would not be this hard, and we both know it," Xander reached up and ran his hand over the stubble lining his jawline. "You're different now and not just with me. I had once believed it was because I had fallen, but Asher informed me that you have been cold with him as well."

I shifted my weight between my feet, uncomfortable with where the conversation was going. "I don't know what you are insinuating,

Xan. I am exactly the same as I have always been."

"No, you are not, and you are beginning to worry everyone." Xander caught my green eyes. "Is it the council?"

I simply nodded at him. The pressure building on top of my chest struck me like I was hit by a semi. Turning my back to Xander, I didn't want him to see me lose control over my emotions. He sidestepped around me, not allowing me to escape his powerful gaze. "Aspyn Jane, if they are pressuring you again, I swear to…"

"To God? I don't think he would appreciate that very much." I let out a watery laugh. "It never stopped, Xander. I've just gotten better at hiding the aftereffects of Abel's mind games. Being forced to work so closely with him has made it worse, but someone has to handle the wing removals. It's only a matter of time before I am forced to act on them. At least Cee is paired with the job most of the time."

Abel found pleasure in assigning me my role with the Elite. I was to record those who had fallen in the archived books and the ones who had survived the wing stripping before delivering them to the Keeper. Along with recording, I was forced to attend every one of the wing removals. The sickening rip of skin haunted my dreams. Abel thought of this as some sick twisted game taking in every ounce of my pain and wielding it into a sport for him to toy with me. He had made me stand and watch Xander be tortured without being able to protest.

Xander wrapped me in his arms. "We all thought you were not required to attend the removals after me. Why did you not say anything?"

"It wouldn't have made a difference," I mumbled into the fabric of his shirt. I could feel the river of tears gathering on the front in giant patches. "Do you understand why I can't put myself in the middle of this?"

"No," he said. I pulled back to look up at him confusion. "I understand why you are scared, but that doesn't give you a reason to abandon your family."

Stepping out of his grip, I wiped the tears from my cheeks. "I guess if one falls, we all fall together, right?"

"That is the Aspyn we all know and love." Xander grinned down at me. He turned, motioning me to follow him down the mountain, but my voice stopped him in his tracks.

"I have one request."

Xander turned back to look at me, one eyebrow quirked up in question as I played my hand. "Finley stays out of this. I refuse to take him down with us."

Chapter Six
Before

A wool blanket was draped loosely over my bare shoulders as I nursed the warm liquid in a yellow enamel mug. I leaned back against Finley, watching the fire spark in front of us. "Our spot" was a large cabin that sat just on the border of town. The only ones aware of its existence were Finley, my brother, and me.

Fin and I had claimed the large study in the front of the cabin. The room was spacious with built-in bookshelves lining every wall but the front one, which was home to a stone fireplace. A large blue couch we'd scavenged from a local garage on a random Saturday morning was placed in the middle of the room. This was the only place we could be ourselves without having to worry about the council scolding us. It was our own slice of heaven in Idelwood.

Light strokes of fingertips ran up and down my exposed leg, which was propped up against the arm rest. My eyes fluttered shut as the electrifying touches turned into a soft hum, lulling my body into sleep it so desperately needed.

Finley's deep chuckle broke me from falling deeper into the black void closing in around me. Peeking through my dark lashes, I leaned my head back to glare up at him. "What?"

"You're drooling." His voice was soft as his fingers stopped the strokes and came up toward the corner of my mouth. I swatted his hand away before it met the drool and quickly wiped it with my sweater sleeve. The action only made him laugh harder. His chest rumbled as I cuddled back down into him, trying to conceal the creeping blush forming on my cheeks.

The wool blanket fell to the side, leaving my collarbone exposed to the chilled air the fire had not fully warmed. Finley moved down, placing his lips on the sensitive skin, causing a shiver to run through me under his whispers. "Asp, you need to rest, or you are going to wear yourself thin."

"I'm fine," I croaked out, trying to hold together my composure as his lips made lazy patterns up my neck and finally landed just below my earlobe. In the second he paused, I turned around, both legs straddling on either side of his hips. The tip of my nose brushed against his as I leaned in. Finley's blue eyes bored into my green ones, waiting for my next move.

It was the first moment since the ceremony that we had been truly alone. My avoidance of everyone had managed to include him as well, even if I hadn't intentionally done it. Ever since I watched the image of Finley appear across the holy water, just being in the same room as him caused my skin to purr louder than it had ever done. From the glazed-over look in Finley's eyes, I could tell that my emotions mirrored his, whether that was because he could feel them coursing through my veins or because he really felt the same way.

"You are a terrible liar." Finley's words brushed

up against my lips, each one tasting sweeter than the last. My body begged me to close the gap between us, but the guilt of what I had agreed to hours beforehand hung heavy in the air.

"Why would I lie to you?" I asked, voice shaking under his stare.

Finley pulled back slightly to get a better look at me, concern plastered across his face. "Aspyn what is going on? You're acting strange, darling."

I smiled at the pet name. He reached up, pushing back a fallen curl hanging in my face. I leaned into his touch. "Nothing. I promise, Fin. The stress of what we know is messing with my head and the fact that Ash still refuses to speak to me. It's been eight days, for heaven's sake. He's never stayed this mad at me for so long."

With a light push, I threw myself backward away from Fin. My head connected with the armrest of the couch, sending a nauseating thud through the room. I moaned out in pain, "I am taking that as a sign karma is on Asher's side right now."

Finley hovered over me, trying his best to hide the laughter which threated to spill from his lips.

"He'll come around. Asher always does. I could talk to him if you want me too."

Groaning once more, I closed my eyes. "No, it will just make everything worse."

I peeked through my eyelashes to look up at the redhead. My bottom lip stuck out in a heavy pout. Finley promptly planted a soft kiss upon my puckered lips. "Okay. Now come back over here."

I propped my elbows up against the cushions. "I have a better idea."

Reaching up, I gripped onto the collar of his white polo and crashed my lips against his. The surprise of the kiss made him stumble, his body almost slamming into me, but he caught himself and placed both hands on the armrest next to my head. Our lips moved in perfect sync, bodies molding together in seamless precision. The bond of the ceremony flowed through our kiss, making each one hungrier than the last. My fingers slid over his shoulders before I dug them into the fabric of the shirt, wishing it would dissipate under my hands. Even through the thick cotton, I could feel the familiar flutter of his wings as they responded to my touch with heavy beats.

The sound of strong hands slamming against the front door jolted us from the kiss. Our heavy breathing fell away as the air in the room was restricted with fear of the unknown presence. Finley stood from the couch ready to investigate the sound, but I caught his wrist and pulled him back to me. A few heavy footsteps rang out in the hallway before the light flicked on, and the study's door swung open to reveal a stone-faced Asher.

"Ash." I stood from my spot, voice cracking in anticipation. *Please be here to talk.* The thought circled around my mind as I stared at my brother. Seeing him after we had been avoiding each other made my heart ache. The sting reminded me how even if we fought constantly, I would never abandon him. I stepped around Fin, a grimace crossing his face as I tightened my grip on his wrist.

Asher's features darkened. "He has requested your presence."

My blood ran cold, knowing if Abel had sent Asher to find me in the middle of the night, it was not a good sign. If this couldn't wait to be handled until morning, whoever was falling tonight had royally messed up in the council's eyes.

And it was not in the council's nature to be forgiving.

My black heels smashed into the marble flooring of the town hall. The building was eerily silent at night, leaving me with an uneasy feeling coursing through my veins. After Asher had announced Abel had summoned me, he fled the cabin without giving me a second glance. Out of all our arguments, this time felt different. This time we may not be able to recover from it, even if I had agreed to Xander's terms hours earlier.

My feet were frozen as I placed my foot on the final step leading up to the council's chamber where the Elite angels of Idelwood gathered to meet daily. The double doors screamed danger to me. I needed time to clear my mind of all things Xander and Rowen if I was to keep my promise to them. Abel would be able to sniff out a lie if I did not shove the secret down into the back of my mind. Right now, there was a job to attend to, no matter how much I hated it. The mere thought of being subpar in this environment was unacceptable. Subpar got you killed or even worse, thrown out in the cold with a new devilish label.

Taking in a final gulp of air, I trudged toward the doors once more and pushed through the wood until they revealed only Abel sitting in his usual seat at the long table. Abel looked up from the papers arranged in front of him to glare at me over wire-rimmed glasses. His gaze scanned over my appearance; I had changed into a more appropriate outfit which included a black pencil skirt and white blouse. My muscles fought against my mind to not squirm under Abel's scrutinization. Finally, after a few moments, his glare landed back on my gaze.

"When I summon you, I should not have to send an errand boy to fetch you, Aspyn." Abel's voice hardened. "This won't happened again. Will it?"

I swallowed, knowing the severity of his question. "No sir, I apologize for my absence."

Abel flicked his wrist toward me, sending a

cream-colored folder sliding across the slick floor to land in front of my feet. "Review that before it is filed. Then report to the hall. The other members will be arriving shortly."

Nodding quickly, I made my way out of the room. A hallway stretched down for what appeared to be miles, lined on each side with offices. I slipped into the third door to the left, where the front of the dark wood held a single metal plate with my name etched into the gold. The plaque had been slipped into its place holder with such a secure grip that even slamming the door behind me would've left it unfazed. I reached out to the right and flicked on the light. It filled the room with a dim yellow tint which sent a sickly aura over the entire space.

My office was a cramped space, only enough room for a large filing cabinet adorned with a black office chair behind it. I tried to spend as little time as possible in there and refused to add any personal artifacts to scatter through the space. It was as if anyone could work in here — the only indication it was occupied by an Elite member was the gold plate slapped onto the door. "A real honor" was what everyone said when I received my position.

Yeah, right.

I threw down the folder and slumped into the uncomfortable plastic of the chair. My eyes just started toward the cream color which had dirty fingerprints pressed into its surface. The papers peeking out of the side held the fate of one unlucky soul. If I could set them on fire and forget they ever existed, I would, but Abel had already gone through the report. He had already made the decision, and it must be bad if we were pulling council members from their beds at this hour.

A clock ticked on the wall, reading just past two in the morning. I placed my hands on the desk in front of me and pulled the chair near the surface. Closer to the ugly truth lying within the folder. Flipping the file open, I found a large red stamp smeared across the page, identifying the angel whose picture lay in the corner of the paper. A sick feeling crashed into me as I caught a glimpse of the image. The bright eyes of Mallory Manson glared back at me.

I knew she had been furious in the moment we had spoken in the Crypts, but even with all the fury the tiny girl held in her, I never thought she would do something so reckless. The air was knocked from my lungs as my thoughts began to spiral about the effects that this would have on the group. Delaney would throw herself into the line of fire if it meant saving the sister she was closest to. No amount of Mal's threatening would stop her siblings from following after her. If it were Asher, nothing would get in my way either.

A sharp knock on the office door broke me from my trance. "Come in."

The words were distant. Every part of me resisted pulling myself from the clenched grip I had on the desk. A figure stepped through the small crack they made with the door: Rowen. She stood tall in a lilac-colored lace dress, ever the beauty. I sucked in another harsh breath, letting the first tears to drop from my eyes.

"What happened?" I whispered. Rowen's face was void of emotions as she stared at me. I slammed my hands against the wooden desk, the entire structure shaking under my touch. "Rowen! What happened?"

My harsh voice pulled her out of the rehearsed face she always wore in front of the council and replaced it with a devastated one. She shook her head. "They won't say anything. The only thing I can be certain of is that it isn't good. I heard whispers of terminating her instead. Never in the thousands of years I've been around has the council or Abel suggested such a thing."

Light clicks of her heels rattled against the floor as she paced back and forth. The motion made my building terror bubble over. Rolling my shoulders back, I continued to watch her travel from one side of the room to the other in seconds. "Where's Laney? She must be about to tear this town apart to get to Mal."

"Asher and Xander intercepted her before she managed to do anything stupid. Even though they hate each other, Tabitha is trying to calm her sister down." I rolled my eyes, earning a glare in return. "We didn't truly have a choice in this situation. They are both trying the best they can."

"I know." I sighed, running one hand over my face. "But Tabby? Honestly those two will level this town being in the same room. Let's just hope Xander hid Laney's box from her."

Rowen let out a watery laugh. "She is not going to poison her sister when the other one is in the hands of Abel."

"I wouldn't push the idea off the table, Row," I shrugged my shoulders as she began to pace once again.

All we could do now was wait for the summoning.

Chapter Seven
Before

The entire room was silent as I made my way into a chamber rarely used. We only gathered there for wing removals, and the screams of previous victims still rung in my ears. Each of the walls were covered in a heavy black curtain which swayed against the breeze coming from a large window on the opposite end of the room. The soft scent of smoke burning through the night air wafted into the space. I peered out the window to see just beyond town square where a soft glow of a roaring fire sat in the middle of the tree line, indicating another wild party was being held by the teens of the small town.

This entire place was just another game to the

Elite. A wicked game no one could escape.

"Do you ever wish you could leave this place, Row?" I turned to look at the girl who stood in the doorway. She waited patiently to greet the council who would soon file in for the sentencing. Her caramel-colored gaze stared intently toward the same town as me.

There was a hint of sadness swimming through the color, but it quickly faded away, leaving only a hardened glare behind. She was careful to hide her emotions just in case Abel and his minions rounded the corner. I had always envied her control that she had always presented. It would make my life so much easier to not show every emotion on my face.

"More and more as the days go on, but we all know that the idea is just a fantasy none of us will have the pleasure of fulfilling." Rowen reached down and laid one hand over her abdomen. I watched her movement intently, and it was as if she didn't even notice her actions, but soon enough, she snapped herself back into reality and ripped her hand away from its spot. Rowen clasped both hands together in front of her, taking the proper greeting position once again.

A loud bang of in sync steps clamored down the hallway before Abel traveled around the corner and into the room. He led the pack of followers he had brainwashed with a wicked smile.

"Ah, lovely Rowen." Abel reached up, placing one of his talons on Rowen's shoulder. She stood perfectly still, but I could see the concentration in her eyes as she tried to not shudder under his touch. His grin grew. "Always a pleasure to have you in these."

Rowen simply smiled and nodded once toward the man, careful not to use her voice. I eyed her, waiting for the undetected signal that she sent my way as Abel traveled toward a chair which sat in the middle of the room. He gripped down onto the backing of it, eyes scanning the entire room. The other council men shuffled in after him, taking their seats in their designated positions. I tried to take in a breath to calm myself down, but the air was too thick, making it impossible to gather enough oxygen to fill my lungs fully.

"Well, I don't know what we are waiting for. Rowen, send them in." Abel rounded the chair to take his seat. He leaned back with an evil smirk of anticipation plastered against his face. Rowen scurried quickly out the door before returning moments later. Her face was void of color, eyes roaming around in horror as they met mine.

I flicked my gaze to the door, counting down the seconds before the footsteps entered, the fear in the room doubling with each moment that ticked by. Two men gripped either side of Mallory Manson as they pulled her through the entrance. Her normally bright blonde hair was matted and dirty while dark purple bruises covered almost every inch of her pale arms, matching the ones circling her eyes. Even under all the damage, Mallory held her head strong without showing an ounce of fear toward the council members. The girl even had the nerve to glare in the direction of Abel. He only returned a sinister smile her way.

"Thank you, boys." Ravana rounded the men, running a nail over each of their shoulders. My gaze left Mallory and landed on the vindictive angel smirking at me. She brought one finger to her red painted lips, hushing my silent threats. "Mallory Manson, yours is a face I never thought I would witness standing before us in this room."

Ravana towered over Mal's tiny frame in black heels that matched the low-cut dress flowing around her ankles in a pool of darkness. Mallory flinched away from Ravana's taunting finger as she ran it underneath the girl's chin.

"Stop teasing the poor creature, Ravana," Rowen's bored voice spoke up. I shuddered under her tone even if it was only a mask to hide the fear, the lack of emotion for the situation stung.

I turned toward Abel, waiting for him to intervene in between the feuding angels, but he just sat there with a sadistic smile and watched as they glared at each other. Ravana's eyes matched the fire in Rowen's like a mirrored reflection. The strawberry-blonde angel stepped forward, lips pulled back in a snarl. The sound made the hairs on the back of my neck stand straight up. Even I knew getting on the Caldwell woman's bad side would never end up well for the other party. Her power was vast—I had witnessed Rowen cause a dove to drop dead in less than a second flat during training.

As Rowen descended on the burgundy-haired angel, Abel stood from his seat. The command was clear, and Rowen flew back into the corner of the room in fear, regaining her control with every step.

"Why are we here, Abel?" a council member at the opposite end of the table spoke up. He was a short man with long lanky arms which hung loosely across his chest. The man's name slipped my mind. Abel was the only one who could strike the fear of the heavens in any creature of Idelwood. It was the only name that was worth remembering.

"Mallory Manon has committed treason against the heavens and hereby is sentenced to the removal of her wings." Abel turned to address his followers, his voice booming and arms flying about in a dramatic show.

"Yes, we all understand that, but what was dire enough that you had us all dragged from our beds in the middle of the night?" a new council member asked. The murmurs of agreement made it impossible for me to track the original source.

"Yes Abel, what did I do?" Mallory taunted the man in front of her, a sly smile showing off a busted lip which had begun to swell in the minutes since she'd walked into the room. A fresh wound, but soon it would be the least of her problems.

Abel twisted back to the broken girl. "You stole an artifact from the Crypts while you were tending to them—a gold medallion which has been in the protection of the Keepers for centuries. It was carved from The Ark of the Covenant and strung into a necklace for those who were chosen to wear it as a form of protection. The necklace is one of the most sacred pieces in Idelwood's Crypt, and she handed it off to Claire Halloway."

I gasped, unable to contain myself. Thankfully most of the council had the same reaction, masking my shock. Mallory didn't flinch at the accusation but instead smiled brighter. "If that is what you believe to be true, Abel, then so be it. Although I do think the Halloway girl is the least of your worries at the moment."

Abel lunged forward, closing the gap between the two of them. He loomed over her even as she stood as straight as her spine would allow. "Get her set."

The men holding Mallory pulled her back from Abel and into the center of the room, slamming her down onto her knees. They made a revolting crunch as they hit the concrete floor, causing me to flinch into my shoulder. Stepping back, I tried to conform into the darkest corner of the room, wanting nothing more than to be suffocated by the black fabric. My sudden movement caught Abel's attention. He cocked him head in my direction, stretching one long finger to beckon me toward the upcoming mutilation.

My feet carried me toward the leader, but my mind stayed hidden in the corner trying to rationalize an easy explanation for his sudden need for me. When I reached him, Abel leaned down, his hot breath brushing against the inside of my ear. "You will pluck the wings from her back."

I felt the color drain from my face. "What?"

Pulling away from him, I stared at the man in

confusion. He spoke once again, but this time to ensure the entire room could hear, "I have decided Aspyn has proven herself as a loyal follower. As a reward for her dedication, she will be performing the wing removal tonight."

A bead of sweat trailed down the back of my neck as I stared blankly at him. This was not my job. I was to deliver the paperwork and attend meetings when summoned. Nothing had prepared me for the idea of ripping out the one thing we loved more than life itself, but if I refused, I would be the next kneeling in front of him. Arms stretched out wide until my beautiful wings burst from my shoulder blades and were torn from my skin.

Nodding at him, I traveled around Mallory and the men to wait for the signal to be given. Abel took his seat and gave a deep smirk before waving his hand to begin.

I felt nothing when the first tear of skin sent a splatter of warm blood across of my face.

Bright red liquid drained down the rusted sink in the small bathroom of the cabin. When everything had been completed, and we were dismissed from the room, I had run. Rowen had tried to stop me, but I maneuvered away from her with hands soaked with the blood of the girl I had grown up with. I had no doubt word had gotten back to both Asher and Finley. It was only a matter of time before they showed up.

I scrubbed at my knuckles, the skin growing raw, but I still felt dirty. If I bled a small bit, I thought it might release the pain which sat low in my heart right now.

The cabin shook as the front door slammed against the wall, signaling one of the boys had arrived or an angry sister was here to take out the revenge she so desired at the moment. Looking up at the mirror, I finally got a good look at myself. Black smudges gathered underneath my eyes, and my skin was pulled so taut that it had a translucent hue. I could see the dark veins which traveled throughout my skin pulsating against my neck. Choking back a sob, I looked back down at the raw skin on my hands. My goal of drawing blood had been achieved, as the dark liquid began to pool out of several small cuts.

"Asp," a cautious voice spoke behind me. I glared down at the cuts, too scared to see who was standing behind me. My eyes traveled up, meeting Asher's through the mirror. His gaze looked haunted as he took me in. I didn't bother turning off the faucet as I turned and launched myself into my brother's arms just as I had when we were children and I'd scraped my knee. But the hurt I felt wasn't a superficial wound that could be sealed with a simple bandage.

Clutching tightly to the dark T-shirt he wore, I sobbed loudly, letting my tears soak into the soft fabric on his shoulder. My knees gave out from under me, but Asher's grip on me held my figure upright, allowing him to lower us to the ground slowly. As we sat in the bathroom doorway, the only sounds audible above my sobs were the water streaming above us and Asher's soft, soothing whispers. I listened to those words until the darkness I was feeling swallowed me whole.

Chapter Eight
Before

Soft clicks of dishware swirled around me when I finally came up from a deep sleep. The blue couch Finley and I had been on earlier felt lumpy this time around as I gazed into the barely lit embers igniting each other in the fireplace. It was the only light filling the room, and the shadows of the space wavered in and out of each other. I swung my legs off the couch, noticing the deep slit running up the side of my once pristine pencil skirt. A red smear ran down the front of my white dress shirt, causing my stomach to roll in disgust. Images of the night's event played in the firelight, taunting me as Mallory's screams broke through the fire's crackles.

I shot up, racing out the door to escape the sounds. My eyes watched the empty darkness, feet still moving in the direction of the commotion in the kitchen. The wood panels refused to let me get a good grip on its slick floor, causing me to skid through the long hall until I smacked into a hard surface. A strong grip caught my shoulders, holding my shuddering figure in place.

"Hey, Asp." A deep raspy voice echoed through the hall, but I refused to look up toward it, eyes still trained on the darkness. I waited for the screams to trail after me, but they never came. The voice's soft touch trailed underneath my chin, pulling my stare away from the room. Finley's concerned eyes watched me carefully. "There you are."

I collided with him, throwing my arms around his neck, and inhaling the familiar sweet smell that only belonged to him. His arms gripped my hips, securing me tightly against him. "Let's get you changed out of that shirt."

Neither of us moved for a moment, too entranced in each other's touch. I unlocked my grip from Finley's neck, pulling away only a few inches to ensure the protection his arms brought did not fade away. Fin simply laid his hand on the small of my back, leading me to a room on the upper level of the cabin. I hadn't spent much time up here, as it had become routine to meet in our space the past few months.

A mattress stretched from corner to corner, filling the entire room with a large bed. Inching past Finley, I threw myself back on to the comforter and stared up at the ceiling. The redhead shuffled around the room before appearing above me holding out new clothing.

I smiled sadly at him and picked up the sweater on the top of the pile. "Thanks."

"Anytime, darling." His words were hushed as he leaned down to brush a kiss between my brows. I sighed, content to just stay here for a few more seconds, but Fin disappeared out of the bedroom door without another word.

Pulling myself up, I ripped the blouse open, allowing buttons to fly in whatever direction they pleased. The shirt was no use to me with the deep crimson stains seeping through the material. Now it was just an ugly reminder of the monster I had become. The blood had seeped underneath the material and onto my skin. I clutched the fresh sweater, curling around the knit fabric as a painful sob escaped my lips.

The door cracked open once again, but this time instead of Fin, it was Rowen who entered. I snapped my mouth shut, furiously wiping my tears away from my eyes. Though I knew she had already seen my crumbled state, I didn't want her or anyone else's pity.

"What are you doing here?" I slipped into the baggy tan sweater. The sleeves hung over my hands, and the sweet citrus scent that lingered on the fabric indicated that it had been recently worn by Finley.

"Finley said you were up here." Rowen shifted her weight uncomfortably between both feet, her eyes never looking directly into mine. "I came to check in on you."

"I'm fine, Row," I said, standing from the bed. The sweater fell toward my knees as I slid off the torn pencil skirt and replaced it with a pair of black pajama shorts. Rowen's calculating eyes watched my movements. "Really, Rowen, you don't have to worry about me. Shouldn't you be lying down or something in your condition?"

Rowen snorted. "I am pregnant, Aspyn, not dying."

"Pretty much the same thing," I mumbled.

"Claire would like to see you," Rowen said softly, causing my head to snap up in her direction. She placed her hands over her stomach, rubbing soothing circles around the swollen skin. In the tight shirt she had replaced her dress with, I could see the signs of the life growing inside her more than ever. If the idea terrified me, the sight of it drove that feeling in more. Rowen caught me staring and smiled. "Did I tell you we knew what we had decided to name her if she was girl before your brother's ceremony ruined the surprise?"

"No." I shook my head. "But Liliana is a beautiful name. I am sure it will suit her well."

"We hope so." She nodded lightly. The two of us let the silence encompass us. Rowen knew any mention of the baby made me uncomfortable.

"You said Claire wants to see me. Do you have any idea why?"

"She would not say, but it seemed urgent." Rowen looked away from me, a strange darkness settling on her features. "Claire said to meet her at the church tomorrow night just before the sun begins to set."

A white, pristine church sat on the other side of a wooden bridge. It was surrounded by a small stream that was flowing rapidly in the harsh wind of the storm brewing above. Lightning illuminated the almost sunless sky and cast a chilling glow over the meeting point.

Claire was a nice girl, a little too curious for her own good but nice all the same. Though she did have an attitude which accompanied her most days, she had always been a light in the middle of the chaos from the second she moved into Idelwood's boundaries. I had always viewed the Halloway girl as harmless to us, but that was before she had the ammunition to take us all down if she ever uttered a word to anyone. Now she could be more dangerous than any one of us on a bad day. The thought frightened me to my core.

I stepped across the bridge and into the small garden which surrounded the church's front doors. It was nothing special, but the flowers that were trying to bloom through the frozen ground gave the old building an inviting atmosphere. After gathering up the courage, I pushed through the double doors and into the worship hall. Everything looked as it did every Sunday when the locals gathered to hear the pastor give his sermon.

On occasion I would sneak off without anyone knowing to sit in the last row by myself and listen to his words. Most points he interpreted wrong, but it still intrigued me to hear how the mortals painted us in their lessons.

"I am glad you could make it, Aspyn." Claire sat in the front row. She had her body turned to face mine and gestured for me to join her. I followed her request, sitting an arm's length away from her, my eyes trailing up to the large glass window that depicted the Garden of Eden in brilliant colors. In the corner of the room, a bowl of holy water which was normally placed in the center of the raised stage sent dots of sunlight across the plaster, making everything in the space feel warm and welcoming to the unsuspecting eye. But the tension rolling off the girl's skin surrounded us in heavy thick clouds.

"Why did you ask to see me, Claire?" I kept my voice even, not allowing it to give away any true emotions that wanted to break through. My gaze stayed pointed forward, but I could see the young girl move her body to face me. Claire watched me curiously, almost as if I was a specimen in a tube, she was discovering for the first time. Even with this new revelation Xander and Rowen had given her, I was still the same Aspyn she had always known. Now she just knew I sprouted wings from my back when I deemed it necessary. Which was hardly ever nowadays.

Claire's melodic laugh broke over the silence. "I have never seen you so serious, Aspyn. If you keep it up, you're going to cause wrinkles. Though I guess since you never age past the prime age you were granted, wrinkles are the least of your worries."

I whipped my head to the side, meeting her cool gaze with a fiery one. "Do you think this is a joke? You knowing about what resides within Idelwood's boundaries puts all—"

"All of us at risk," she interrupted. "Xander already gave me this speech after Rowen broke it down for me. We all know and understand the risks, Aspyn. You don't have to keep repeating them to anyone who will listen."

Claire twisted behind her, causing the sun shining through the glass window to catch the gold medallion hanging between her breasts. I gulped down the bile which had begun to rise in my throat. That was the item which had cost Mallory her wings. The hands that plucked her like a chicken began to shake violently. Shooting out of my seat, I staggered away from the Halloway girl. She looked up in surprise, not grasping why I fled from my spot on the pew.

"Aspyn?" Claire stood from her spot as well. She stepped closer to me, and I matched it with one of my own backward. "I didn't mean to upset you.

Rowen just thought if I told you myself what we had decided that you would take the news better."

"Did you know? That Mallory would lose her wings when they saw what hangs around your neck?" I spoke in shaky breaths that rocked through my entire body. Claire's eyes traveled down toward the gold trinket, bringing one finger up to brush its metal surface.

"No," Claire whispered. "Mallory brought the necklace to me and told me it was important that I wore it. She specifically commanded me to never take this ugly thing off. When she had fallen, I was shocked. We all were. I still don't truly understand the purpose of wearing it."

"It is for protection. Mal knows the power it holds. If you pass it down to Liliana once she is born, no angel or fallen will be able to harm her or remove it without severe consequences."

"What would happen if one of your kind tried?"

"Hellfire. It would incinerate them before they even registered what was occurring," I said with as much conviction as I could muster.

"When was the last time you spoke to your

brother?" Claire asked. Her sudden change of subject took me by surprise. Asher and I hadn't truly spoken since the fight we had in the clearing. Last night's escapade with the council might have thawed the thick tension between us, but I knew the fight was long from over.

"Is that why you came to speak with me?"

"You could say that." Claire's mouth twitched up into a sly grin. "Asher came to me, you see. I thought it was odd no one accompanied him when I have rarely seen him without you or your lover Finley trailing behind him."

I turned my glare back on her. "We had a disagreement, but that is none of your concern, Claire, and keep Finley's name out of your mouth."

She chuckled darkly. "Oh yes, I forget Xander told me how protective you were of him. Informed me that Finley was to partake in no part of this mess we are all about to stir up in this town."

"*We?* No, there is no we in this. I agreed to protect the child, not start a civil war with the council," I hissed toward her. Turning away from the girl, I began to walk down the long rows of pews.

"But isn't that what Liliana is? A child who should never exist cannot be hidden in the shadows forever. She will be the death of both Heaven and Hell combined."

Chapter Nine
Before

Claire's words sparked a flame inside my soul that I had not known was there before. I stalked back through the forest to the edge of town. The streets were crowded with locals who had just departed from their mundane jobs. Shoving my way through the crowd, I managed to make my way to Celia's café, which was flooded with customers who had a craving for her southern cooking.

The scent of freshly seasoned chicken and fried potatoes wafted through the cool air of the café. My eyes scanned the building trying to find the blonde-haired woman who hid behind her southern charm, but the smiling face of Emaline

Chadwick averted my vision from her.

"Aspyn." Emma gathered me in a friendly hug that I did not return. She pulled back, not seeming to notice my rigid stance. "How have you been? I didn't see you after your ceremony to congratulate you and Finley. After what happened with Asher, I assumed everyone was in a bit of disarray."

Her arm nudged mine and I gave her a tight-lipped smile in response. "Yeah, everything got pretty insane after that."

"But I assume everything is figured out?" Emma pried. I nodded once, making sure to keep my emotions at bay. "We need to catch up soon, maybe at my bridal shower? Rowen said she will come, but just between the two of us, she's been acting strangely. Will says it's nothing but the usual Rowen mood swings we have seen."

"Yeah, she is just under a lot of pressure." I trailed off, catching Cee's eyes from across the room as she disappeared into the back room. "Look, I have to speak with Celia, but just let me know when the shower is, and I will be there."

Maneuvering around Emaline, I didn't bother

waiting for her to respond. I stumbled toward the swinging door Celia had just pushed through. The backroom was divided into two separate hallways, one leading to the door of Cee's home and the other to the café's back stock room. Chill air drifted around me as I stepped in between the metal shelves on either side of the hall.

"Cee?" I called into the empty air. After a few moments her head popped around the corner of a shelf which held large bags of flour and baking soda.

"What's got you flying off the handle, sugar?" She squinted at my frazzled face. In her hands were individual saran wrapped containers of vegetables she was storing in the cooler to her right.

"Claire Halloway," I gritted out. The name made the hair on the back of my neck stand up. "She learned about everything, and after just a few days, she believes herself to be an expert on all things angel-related in Idelwood."

"She always did seem to be that type." Celia rolled her eyes and went back to her task in the cooler. I followed after her and watched as she stacked the veggies back in their respective places. "What did she say that got you so worked up? You aren't one to let someone's words bother you so much. Not unless that someone is Asher or Finley, that is."

She gave me a cheeky smile. I rolled my eyes at the woman. "Claire thinks that this devil child that Rowen and Xander have produced is going to the destruction of every single one of us."

"Well, could she be telling the truth?" Celia shooed me from the cooler, shutting the door behind her.

My brows scrunched in confusion. "The truth? Celia, she only just found out about us, and you're insinuating that she has the knowledge to predict our future?"

"I have heard crazier notions these days." Celia shrugged in response. "Plus, a little birdy told me she knew before Xander spilled the beans."

Before I could respond to the nonsense that Celia had just uttered, a large crash of metal reverberated off the stone walls surrounding us. I whipped my head in the direction of the commotion, my eyes locking with the horrified look of Emaline. Her mouth bobbed up and down like a fish gulping in its last breath.

"Rowen is pregnant?" Emaline's voice was a breathy whisper. In two long strides, I had her forearm clenched in my grip.

I glared down at her. "What are you doing back here?"

"I forgot to give you this," she choked out, cowering under my stare. In her hand was a cream envelope with my name scrawled across the front. The handwriting was not recognizable as I examined it closer. I snatched it out of her shaking hand. "I swear I won't tell anyone about this, Aspyn."

"How do I know you're telling the truth? You are engaged to a council member in training," I spat venomous words at her. She stepped back into the metal rack, trying her best to put some distance between us.

"Rowen is my best friend. Do you think so lowly of me that you'd expect me to rat her out?" Emma spoke with a confidence I had never heard from her. I shook my head, debating what I was to do with this.

"Aspyn." Celia pulled my attention from my thoughts. I had almost forgotten she was watching the entire interaction. "Do not do something you're going to regret in a few hours, sugar."

Her soft, motherly tone calmed my anger slightly, but I had no choice in the matter. Xander had to know. Nodding once at the woman, I didn't dare utter a word that she could use to convince me against my decision. I reached out, gripping Emaline once more, and began to pull her toward the emergency exit door just behind Celia.

Celia caught me by the back of my leather jacket, her motherly touch gone and replaced with the fierce Keeper she was. "I can't allow you to harm her."

"What? You are going to hurt me?" Emaline began to struggle against my grasp.

"Shut up," I hissed through clenched teeth, digging my nails into her arm to force her to stop squirming. Turning my attention back to Cee, I said, "I am not going to hurt her, but she has to go see him."

The sun was almost out of the sky as I pulled Emma after me through the tree line of Idelwood. She kept her mouth shut, not daring to utter a word. It was probably the smartest decision she had made all day. After a few more minutes of silence, we reached the middle of the clearing, and Emaline let out a soft whimper.

"What are you going to do with me?" Her voice was like that of a child who had gotten scolded for having their sticky fingers in the cookie jar.

Flipping my bangs out of my eyes, I scoffed at her accusation. "I am not going to do anything to you, Emaline."

"Then why did you bring me out here?" Emma's voice was a high-pitched screech. She tried to make a dash for the clearing's edge, not realizing that it was in the wrong direction. I sprinted after her and launched my body toward her. We hit the ground in a painful heap of limbs.

"Would you calm down, you insufferable twit?" I scrambled around her, trying to pin down her arms above her head to stop her from falling off the side of the cliff just in front of us.

"No," she screamed, clawing at the ground to get away from me. "You are all crazy. Every single one of you in this little cult Asher runs."

I barked out a laugh at the idea of Asher ordering any of us around. Swinging one leg from the muddy ground, I straddled either side of Emaline's hips to keep her in place, "Yeah right. Asher has no authority over me."

Emma managed to wiggle her way out from under me. Her sneaker came up in the process and connected with my rib cage. The blow sent me tumbling backward, and I gasped for air. She only made it a few more feet in front of me before I latched my hand on her ankle, pulling her back down toward me.

"Aspyn, leave the poor girl alone." Xander's voice boomed around us as the first strike of thunder crashed against the gloomy sky.

I craned my neck to look at him, but he wasn't alone. He had brought the one person I told him I did not want involved in this mess.

Finley's eyes burned with rage as he watched me stand from the forest floor. I reached up, swiping away the dirt that was caked on my face, but I could tell it did nothing. Turning my eyes on Xander, I said softly, "What is he doing here?"

"Xander told me everything." Finley's voice felt like ice burning though my soul. I took a silent step back, trying to escape his rage. "Did you really believe that you could hide this from me, Aspyn?"

"I thought I could keep you out of it for as long as I felt necessary, Fin," I mumbled, my eyes falling to his feet. I couldn't look him in the eye. It hurt me to see that he was upset with my choices — though I did not regret them. In fact, I would do it again if necessary.

"Xander." Emaline's voice shook as she stood. Her eyes never wavered from the fallen angel's captivating ones. I had almost forgotten the real reason I had called him here. "What is going on? Aspyn said tha—"

"Aspyn misspoke." Xander's cold eyes watched mine. "She has been feeding lies to others in town. It is just a plot to remove Rowen from the council."

"I would never," I said, voice hardening at the lies that Xander was spewing. "But please go ahead, believe the devil who is disguised as an angel."

Emma flicked her head between Xander and me until I thought she was going to be sick from whiplash. I traveled forward ready for this conversation to be over with. My shoulder connected with Xander's bicep, and I was halted mid-step by his hand.

"Remove your hand, Alexander," I spat out, words cold as ice as they flooded the silent forest. He flinched, but I stood my ground, waiting for him to unhand me.

"I will come to deal with you later." Xander's warning was low and even. I looked up at him, gasping as I caught sight of the pitch-black eyes looking at me. He claimed to only use his unholy powers against those who he deemed a threat.

"There is nothing more to handle, Alexander. You just made it quite clear that I am not longer a part of whatever this twisted family was. Have fun bringing every one of us down to hell with you."

I ripped myself from his touch, tears beginning to burn the corners of my eyes. Finley stepped forward to guide me back down the dark trail. I waved him off, rushing into the shadows alone.

Chapter Ten
Before

The wood of the front door hit the wall behind it as I stormed through the home's entrance. Asher was summoned out of his room to see what had disturbed the peace. I looked up at him as he draped both arms over the banister and lazily stared down at me.

"To what do I owe the pleasure of your arrival home, sister?" Asher mocked me. It appeared the tense air which had been surrounding us for the past few weeks had dissipated with his playful banter. Although I had a funny feeling it would come back full force once Asher caught wind of what had occurred tonight.

Scoffing at him, I began up the staircase ready

to hide in my room until I was forced out. I reached the top of the landing and turned to the hall, but Asher planted himself in my way. He was watching me with concern, and the look in his eyes told me he knew something was wrong behind my silence.

"What has got you in such a sour mood, Asp?" His voice was soft. "Is it Finley? Do I need to talk to him?"

Rolling my eyes at him, I attempted and failed to step around him. "No, it isn't Fin."

That was only a half truth. If Finley wanted to believe in the lies Xander had crafted for Emaline Chadwick, then so be it. He would learn soon enough the pain choosing Xander would bring him.

"Did I do something to tick you off even more?" Asher asked carefully. I shook my head at him, not trusting my voice to respond. He sighed, running one hand over his jaw in annoyance, but he was doing his best to conceal it. "Then what is it? I am not going to stand here all night and pry it out of you."

"Then don't," I snapped. Asher's eyes widened

at my tone, and he took a cautious step forward to examine me. I turned away, ready to make a quick getaway down the stairs, but he caught me by the arm before I could I squirm out of his touch. "What is it with everyone forcing me to stay in a conversation I so clearly want to escape from?"

Asher flinched away from me like I had burned him with my words. "Aspyn, what is going on with you?"

"I messed up, Ash." I crumbled at those words, allowing a few tears to fall down my face in large droplets.

"I was venting to Cee about Claire Halloway this afternoon, and now Emaline Chadwick knows because she was listening to our conversation." I sucked in a deep breath as Asher's green eyes darkened at my words. "I called Xander right away and thought he would fix it, but he just made things worse."

"Worse for him or you?" Asher's tone was deadly calm, and it terrified me for a split second before I remembered who I was speaking to. This was my brother, and even if I royally messed up, I could always count on him to be by my side.

"He told Emaline I was making up lies about Rowen as a revenge plot I had devised to turn the council against her," I said, my entire being shaking with rage as the moments flitted through my mind like a stop-motion film. "The worst part is that he told Finley, and I think for a moment he believed the lies."

"You know that can't possibly be true," Asher spoke softer this time. He reached out, pulling me into a tight hug. I let out a broken sob into his shoulder, just letting my twin brother hold me for a moment. The crash of the door slamming open caused us to jump apart and peer down at the intruder. Xander stood in the middle of the foyer with Finley, who trailed behind him like a wounded puppy.

"Aspyn," Xander called up to me. He started to make his way up the stairs, but Asher pulled me behind his back before the fallen angel could get any closer.

"You can leave now, Xander." Asher's voice was fierce and hostile as he spoke. I looked around the banister and down at Finley, who was watching me with a guilty expression.

"It was the only way to get Emaline to not speak out against us. Unless you would rather have her death on our hands?" Xander said, making his way to the top of the stairs. I retreated until I could watch the interaction from the corner of the hallway.

"It's also a one-way ticket for Aspyn to lose her wings. Did that ever occur to you?" Asher hissed out through clenched teeth.

Finley's voice reverberated against the walls in the silence. "You mean you were willing to risk Aspyn's soul for your own selfish reasoning?"

"What is wrong with you?" I whispered, but none of males reacted to the sound.

"I would risk the entire world's souls to keep both Rowen and Liliana safe, boy." Xander's eyes caught mine this time as he spoke words which broke me apart even more than the last ones.

"What is wrong with you?" I screamed out and charged forward to stand tall against the fallen angel. "How dare you take my fate into your hands, Alexander! Just because I don't approve of the decisions that are being made around me does not give you the right to make decisions that would damn me for all of eternity."

A crack sounded in the silent hall as my hand connected with Xander's cheek. "Get out. I never want to see you again, Xander."

"Aspyn," Xander pleaded as I retreated to my bedroom. As the door shut behind, I could hear Finley speak up for all of us.

"This child is tearing us apart, Xander. I know you want to protect her, but try to remember who was the first to be at your side the night you fell, and now look who will never be there again because of the broken hero complex you have."

Chapter Eleven
Before

It had been months since I had spoken to either of the Caldwell's. We had come to an unspoken agreement that we would distance ourselves. The heat of the summer months had allowed me to lock myself away in the comfort of an air-conditioned room. Now the heat was melting away into a fall bliss. Trees just outside bloomed with vibrant reds and oranges, and I knew I would have to venture back into society once again.

Finley and I made up later that evening—it was silly for me to believe I had any self-control to stay angry with him.

Shadows bounced off the ceiling of my bedroom as I watched the moonlight come in and out of the windowpanes. Hours of this constant staring had passed before my door finally creaked open to reveal Finley. He stood in the doorway waiting for me to grant him permission to enter. When the words never came, he slipped into the room silently and lay next to me on the plush rug laid across my floor.

"Did you really think I was capable of such evil?" I spoke first, wanting to know the truth that had shuffled around his brain in those revealing moments.

Finley turned to lie on his side, one arm propping his head up so he could look down at me. "No. I had no idea he had intended to use your loyalty as a weapon to deceive Emaline. Though I will not lie — I was angry with you for trying to hide your involvement with the plans to give Claire the child."

My nose scrunched up in confusion, and I turned to meet Finley's gaze. "Give Claire what?"

"Xander explained Claire was to inform you of the proposal to give Liliana to her after the birth. He and Rowen would meet her after they were able to flee town. Xander said you had agreed to help them, but he promised to not involve me."

I sighed, placing my head back into the carpet. "I

never agreed to that. Xander believes that agreeing to keep their secret is a gateway to take advantage in every plot he develops."

"I apologize for my anger against you, Aspyn." Finley leaned down and placed a soft kiss on my hairline. I breathed in contentedly and turned into his embrace. It was all the acknowledgment I could give him in that moment without breaking down once more.

The light sound of rainfall tapped against my bedroom window as I sketched mindlessly on a notepad. My legs were draped over Finley's as he read yet another classic novel I had never heard of. I kept peeking up at him through my eyelashes waiting for him to catch me in the act.

"I know what you are trying to do, darling." Finley kept his eyes on the page in front of him. "And it is not going to work."

"I'm not doing anything." I scoffed at him and went back to my doodles.

"Hm, is that so?" Finley's voice was right next to my ear. I turned my chin up to meet his gaze.

"Yes, it is," I purred and leaned in slowly to trace my lips against his. Just as my lips fully met his, a loud knock against my door broke us apart.

I groaned, "Come in."

Turning to the door as it swung open, I looked upon a figure I had not seen since their wings had been ripped out by my own hands. Mallory Manson stood tall in my doorway. Her vibrant gray eyes didn't look unnatural on her face. Not like Xander's blue ones did. I shuddered at the memory of skin ripping with each tug of my hand. Finley laced his fingers with mine and gave a gentle squeeze to remind me I wasn't back there.

"Mallory." My voice shook slightly as I spoke, "What are you doing here?"

"Asher sent me to come and retrieve you," Mallory spoke softly. Her voice was the same deviously sweet one that I had always known. But now it had a hint more confidence behind it.

Standing from the windowsill seat, I straightened out my T-shirt and began to search for the jacket I had tossed across the room earlier. "Is he alright?"

"I cannot answer that for certain," Mallory said. My eyes flicked up toward her. "He said to have you meet him in the church with Claire Halloway when the sun is at its lowest point."

The girl nodded in acknowledgment to Finley and then fled out of the room with a slight bounce in her step. I craned my neck to watch her until she was out of sight. When I turned back to Finley, his face was a mask of confusion.

"So, I'm not the only one who thought that was strange?" I said, throwing a thumb in the direction of where Mallory just stood.

Finley shrugged. "I just didn't think Asher was into blondes."

Shoving his shoulder slightly, I let out a giggle. "You know there is nothing going on between them."

"But it made you laugh." He beamed down at me. "What I was really thinking was that I didn't know he was still hanging around Xander and his gang of misfits anymore."

"I didn't ask him to choose between me and what he believes his destiny is."

Wind whipped violently around me as I stood staring at the church building. It was a strange place for Asher to ask to meet, but I had an inkling that the real person who requested the meeting was the Halloway girl. Stepping around the wooden bridge, I made my way into the warmth of the space. Altar candles flickered at the front of the room, casting an orange glow across the space. Asher sat in the front section, but Claire was nowhere to be seen.

The sound of my boots clicking against the tiled floor made Asher turn to look at me. He smirked slightly before speaking. "You came."

"Did you not think I would, brother?" I questioned, taking my seat to the right of him.

He chuckled. "I wasn't sure since I had to send Mallory." Flinching at the girl's name, I turned to look at him. Asher's face was twisted up in pain. "Sorry about that. It was either her or Delaney. Mal insisted on going."

"It's fine." I wrung my fingers together as the nerves settled in my stomach. Gulping down the doubt that whispered in the back of my mind, I spoke once more. "So, where is the preacher's daughter? I assume she is the one who requested to speak with the two of us."

"She'll be here." Asher turned to look at the closed doors of the church. "Claire said she had something important to tell us but wouldn't say what it was unless you were here."

"Of course, she wouldn't," I grumbled, my eyes rolling into the back of my head. The wind outside had picked up in violent howls which caused the shutters of the windows to fly open. My ears trained on a terrified scream that rang out over the commotion. Whipping my head around, I stared at the door. "Ash, what was that?"

"It sounded like Claire," Asher said in a hushed tone. Our eyes met before we scrambled off the pews and toward the exit. I pushed on the door, but it didn't budge. Once again, I tried to pry the wood open, and still nothing occurred. Asher pushed me out of the way. "Move back."

I stepped away from the door just in time for Asher to slam his body weight into the it. The wood splintered, flying in every direction. We both charged out of the church but were met with a clear night sky. Not a single tree swayed back and forth in the dead air.

"What the hell was that?" I ran a hand through my dark hair. Asher turned his head from side to side trying to find the source of the scream that had pierced our ears moments before.

"I have no idea, but we need to get out of here," Asher reached down to grip my hand and began to pull me through the rugged woods. "You are probably going to hate me for this."

I gawked at him. "Hate you for what exactly?"

Asher released his hold on me to slip his hand into his back pocket. A sliver cellphone flipped open quickly and he pressed it against his ear. There were a few moments of silence before he spoke, "Xander, we have a problem."

Chapter Twelve
Before

"Have you lost your damn mind?" I screeched at Asher as soon as his call ended. My brother ignored me, starting to walk farther into the forest. I stood staring at him for an instant, not registering that he was truly serious about going to see the man who had threatened my wings just months earlier. Just the thought of being in the same room as him made my vision flash red with rage. "I am not going with you."

Asher whipped around, fury burning in his green eyes. "Like hell you aren't, Aspyn! If I have to throw you over my shoulder as you scream to the heavens, I will."

Folding my arms over my chest, I laughed

darkly at him. "You wouldn't dare."

"Do not test me, sister," Asher spit out. He was always one to be protective, but this was something entirely different. The only entity that would rock him this far over the edge would be the council. I spun around on my heels to head back into the sanctuary and away from him, but another high-pitched scream sounded around us. My hands flew up, pressing into the side of my head as pain ricocheted through it.

"Aspyn!" Asher shouted. I could barely make out the sound of his voice over the wailing. The weight of my body collided with the ground but not before I could threw my hands out to stop myself. Digging my nails into the grass and dirt underneath me, I prayed for the screaming to stop. And then it did.

"What the hell was that?" I panted, trying to rationalize the events that had just occurred.

"I don't know, but this proves my point. We need to get to Xander as soon as possible." Asher looped his arms under mine and hauled me back to my feet. "Are you all right to walk?"

I pushed past him, legs feeling like jelly, but I refused to take his offer for help. Asher followed silently behind me until we reached the main road that connected back into town. I could see the twinkle of glowing lights that lined either side of the square.

"Which way are we headed?" I turned toward my twin. He jutted his head to the left, the opposite way of town. My eyebrows scrunched together in confusion. I had never been out of the city limits. It was forbidden by the council without an explicit assignment that deemed a trip necessary, but those rarely occurred.

"What—are you scared of a little rebellion, Aspyn?" Asher's lips quirked up to send me a devious smile.

Headlights at the end of the road streamed together with the darkness as Asher and I headed in their direction. I prayed that whoever was behind the wheel was not a certain devil I had grown to resent.

"Stop making that face," Asher scolded. "It's not him."

"Who is it then?"

The car's tires came to a stop in front of us. The stranger behind the wheel could not be seen in the darkness of the windows. Throwing one last look behind me at the brightly lit town, I took a breath and swiftly entered the backseat of the vehicle. The warmth of the car surrounded me, and I shut my eyes for a moment as it embraced me. A soft sigh flooded out of my lips.

"You sure you want to do this, Princess?" a rough voice spoke over the quiet. I snapped my eyes open, meeting the piercing gray ones of Delaney Manson. Her cold gaze sent a chill down my back.

"Delaney." I stuttered out her name, ignoring the bile rising in my throat. She sneered at me with such hatred that I almost considered jumping out of the car and running back into town. The slam of the passenger side door startled me out of my thoughts.

Asher angled himself toward Delaney. "Leave her alone, Ice Queen."

Delany shifted her glare to my brother. Even

with Asher trying to match the intensity in her eyes, he failed miserably. Delaney had pent up so much anger in her body that it cut through him like a blade. He flinched away, shifting his back against the seat of the car. Guilt filled the tight, confined space of the car as tears began to pool in my eyes. My hand shot out, gripping down tightly on the door handle to escape the wrath of the Manson girl.

"Don't," Delaney snapped. "It's not worth getting caught wandering back into town. Ask Mallory—she would know all about the consequences and the heathenistic talents she received by your hands alone."

I sank deep into the leather seat, praying to disappear in it with my shame. The rest of the drive was silent, and I kept my eyes trained on the same ripped piece of leather on the back of Delaney's seat. As the minutes ticked on, I could feel us travel further away from the only home I had ever known on earth and onto a dirt path. A rush of adrenaline coursed through my veins as a giddy sensation of what we were doing became a reality.

The tires screeched to a fluid halt, and I pushed myself out of the car as soon as the opportunity presented itself. Asher was right behind me, both of us moving at the same moment to a metal trailer. It was canopied by rising evergreens from the surrounding forest. I could tell this was somewhere that only people who had the right coordinates would be able to find. A perfect place for a demon to lurk in the shadows without the crowned king finding him.

"Come on." Asher flicked his head toward the trailer. "I am sure everyone is waiting impatiently for us."

Hastily I followed close behind him, my nose almost brushing against his shoulder blades. Delaney hung back, her arms coming to rest on the tops of the glossy paint of the car. If she and I could stay a good distance away from each other, we might just be able to make it out alive. And that was a big maybe. My brother stalked up the metal staircase, each step rusted with age. They dipped so much I was sure one wrong step could cause them to snap in half. The metal of the door let out an ominous squeak that carried through the silent wind whipping my hair about.

I halted in the doorway, thoughts of my last interaction with Xander swirling around my mind. It had been months, but the bubbling anger I felt that night flooded my senses. Asher traveled further into the darkness, leaving me in the entry way.

"He has been beating himself up ever since that night," Delany called out toward me. I turned to meet her eyes. She began to venture up the steps, starting into the dark entryway behind me with unwavering eyes.

"I'm sorry for what I did to your sister," I said, the words coming out in a single breath. She snapped her eyes toward me, smoky gray ones shining bright with fresh tears. I had never seen Delaney Manson cry, but the past year had been one full of unseen aspects of life. Delaney only nodded once before shouldering her way past me and into the trailer.

The bottom of my boots felt glued to the metal

porch, extending out into the dark forest. I heard a rustle I could only assume was an animal traveling through the trees, but as my eyes adjusted, I caught sight of movement that looked human. It traveled in one fluid motion toward the gravel road we had just driven on minutes earlier.

Then the movement stopped, turning to lock eyes with me. All I could concentrate on were the vibrant glowing green eyes that menacingly stared me down. Taking a step closer to get a better look made the figure dash away from its place and deeper into the forest. The only indication that it was truly human was the string of inky black hair that whipped around the tree branches.

My breath hitched in the back of my throat as fear washed over me. Whoever or whatever that was had the ability to run back to the council and inform them of the three little angels who thought they could slip from Idelwood without being caught. Turning on my heel, I raced into the tiny hallway that led straight into what looked like a makeshift living room.

A faded brown couch stretched across the entire

space, leaving little room for anyone to pass by either side. The swish of light brown hair billowed around the corner of one of the arm rests. Claire Halloway laid sleeping, her lips moving with silent words from a dream. She looked peaceful, and though I had immense anger toward the odd human who took in our secrets without any hesitation, I was envious of her. Jealous of the fact that she could walk away from us and Idelwood without the fear of being turned into a monster. Claire had freedom, something I never had.

"Aspyn." Rowen's soft musical voice broke through the silent room. Craning my neck to the doorway of the adjoining room, I spotted her hidden in the shadows. Her strawberry-blonde hair was dull in the poorly lit room, and the dark circles hanging under her eyes looked as if she hadn't slept in decades. But that wasn't where my eyes lingered. They stared at her protruding stomach, swollen with life that should have never existed.

"Rowen," I choked out her name. She took a small step forward, trying to close the distance between us.

"Everyone is waiting in the kitchen." She jerked her thumb in the direction of an illuminated room just behind her. I followed her footsteps, a sinking feeling lingering around me with each one. The small kitchen was barely big enough for two people, let alone the six bodies we had crammed in here.

"Aspyn, oh my—" A body collided with mine, knocking the air from my lungs. The heavy scent of vanilla infiltrated my senses, and I knew exactly who has crashed into me. Mallory gripped my shoulders in a bone-crushing hug. I let out a dry sob that could not be stifled in the muffled fabric of her sweatshirt. My arms finally snaked around her middle and squeezed her as hard as she did to me. Even with the earlier interaction, this felt like the first time I was seeing her. Before was so formal it made my skin crawl, but now with the layers peeled back there was no denying the facts.

"I am so sorry, Mal," I whispered, voice watery from the tears that streamed down my face. Mallory pulled away immediately, looking at me with a baffled look.

"What are you apologizing for?" she questioned. "For ripping out my wings? It was either you or Ravana, and I would have much rather you did the deed."

I stared at her, eyes wide and mouth hanging open in shock. Mallory had always been the strongest out of all of us. Every one of us knew that. It wasn't just because she was the one who fixed every minor inconvenience we had, but because she never let the negatives overtake her life. Mallory was fiercely loyal and someone who would lay down her life for the ones she loved. I admired her strength in all aspects of her life.

My head bobbed up and down in a slow motion, finally understanding her side of the entire situation. I allowed my eyes to travel around the room, and *he* was the last one I caught sight of. Xander watched me intently. I sank back from his hardened look, head dropping down to hide. Wandering into the other corner of the room where Asher stood, I hoisted myself onto the small countertop next to the stove.

Xander cleared his throat. "The council has been made aware of Liliana. It will become a witch hunt from here on out to find Rowen and me. There is only so much evading we can do before they catch wind of our location."

"None of us are going to let that happen." Asher's voice was rough when he spoke. I could feel the anxious tension pulsating off him. He had expressed his concerns to me months ago with the question of whether what he was doing was right. Liliana was the soul connected to his, but he had reservations about it. Right now, his concerns were centered around Rowen and Xander's safety. If the child survived after this, we would handle that mess at a later date.

Xander ran his hand down his face, pulling the skin taut as he went, "I don't think we have much of a say in how or when they will come. It is now a question of how we protect her."

Her.

He was not speaking of Rowen, but of the child that had become the destruction of us all. Maybe Claire had made a point in her strange phrase that day in that church. Liliana Caldwell would be the destruction of both heaven and hell. It was only a matter of which side I would be on when the devastation rained down.

The conversation continued in front of me, but I tuned out their bickering. The constant sounds of their voice droned on until the only interesting thing in the room was a chipped tile that was placed on the wall beside Rowen.

"Well, Princess over there hasn't given any mind-bending ideas." Delaney's voice snapped me out of my daze. She stood glaring at me. "Are you going to just sit there and stare or do you think you could use your brain for once in your life to help us?"

"I don't know what you want me to suggest," I snapped at her.

"Aspyn," Xander warned, but I refused to make eye contact with him. "If you have any ideas of how to keep both of them safe and get Claire out of Idelwood with the child, we need to know them. But if not, you are free to leave."

His right hand extended toward the dark room

where Claire slept. I narrowed my eyes at him, refusing to give him the satisfaction of watching me cower from the fight.

"It is not that I am not being forthcoming with my ideas. Unfortunately, it's just that the one who is asking for them stabbed me in the back once before." I hopped off my spot on the counter and strolled over to where he stood. His tall figure towered over me, fury blazing in his stare as he looked down on me. It was the same fire that licked the inside of my veins at the moment.

"You see, Xander, karma is a cruel mistress and a bargain with her is not something that can be made."

Chapter Thirteen
Before

Cool air nipped at my heels as I retreated from the trailer. I had plenty of reasons to be cruel to Xander, but it still made my skin crawl with disgust. This man who dug down to the deepest scars to wound others made it so easy to hurt him back.

The trailers door squeaked open once again, and I waited for the blow of Asher's words to pummel into me like an avalanche of sharp stones. But the voice that came was not one that matched my brother's.

"He deserved that," Mallory's sickly-sweet voice said. "And I think he wants to believe he doesn't, but he does. Xander had no right to do what he did to you."

"I feel that there is a *but* that is needed to be added to the end of your sentence." I turned to look at Mal. Her blonde hair flew around her face.

"But"—her mouth quirked up in a smirk—"that does not mean you should take out the anger you feel for Xander on a child who never asked to be special."

"What do you suppose I do, Mallory? Storm into a meeting and demand they retract their judgment on the child? You know that it would do no good for any of us to stick ourselves in the center of this."

"I have nothing else to lose, Aspyn, which means my idea of sticking my neck out for the ones I love dearly is quite different from your own." Mallory's words floated around me in a quiet whisper. I flinched away at the flashes of bloodied-feather memories that filled my vision. "I don't mean to upset you with my words; I only want to convey that this life isn't as horrific as the council makes it out to be."

"You like being a monster?" I giggled at her

pinched together features.

"I guess you could say that." Mallory nudged her shoulder into mine. "Now, spill. How would you play this if you were one calling the shots?"

I sighed, running a clammy hand against my chest. It would be a lie if I told her I hadn't given this plan a thought. My nightmares were filled with the failed attempts every night, dark stains of blood and feathers scattered at the end.

"Claire has to disappear before the child is born," I began. "If she vanishes the night of the birth, Abel will put the pieces together immediately. The council will send out their best to find her once the medallion is passed down to Liliana. There is also Nathaniel to be taken into consideration. He must accompany Claire as well. He has to be what—nine or ten now?"

Mallory chuckled and shook her head from side to side. "He just turned seven, Asp."

"Oh." I puckered my lips, trying to rack my brain for the last image I had of the boy. "Well, that is beside the point. He'll need to leave with Claire as well."

"These are all things we understand, sister," Asher's voice called from behind me. I turned to observe him leaning against the doorway of the trailer. My rambling words must have distracted me from noticing the door opening. "If you would get on with your point, we might actually be able to get somewhere."

I scoffed at him. "All I am saying is that we are going to need a grand distraction to get all three of them far enough away from here without tipping off Abel."

"Are you suggesting a social gathering?" Mallory asked.

"No." Asher's smirk deepened. "She is suggesting a festival of madness. One that even the council cannot deny being entranced by."

we are dying to see you

Idelwood's
FALL CARNIVAL

Location: Town Square
Time: Dusk

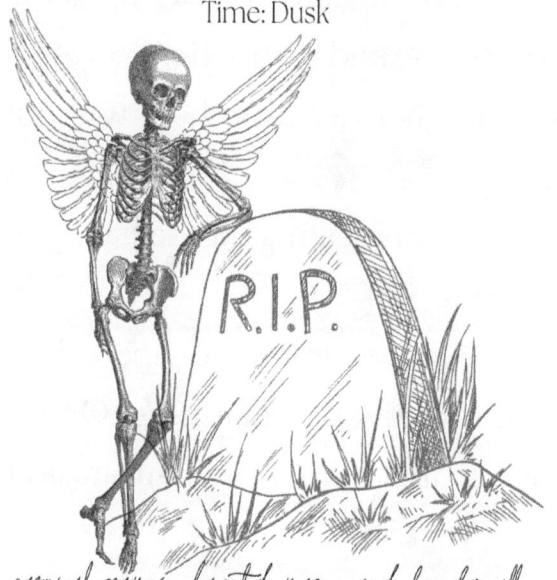

carnival games, haunted maze, and fun for all

ADMISSION TICKET

October 22

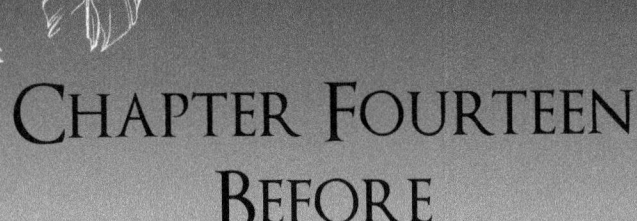

Chapter Fourteen
Before

The stage was set. Mallory had rushed directly to Xander with the plan once we finished speaking. It was decided that I was to bring the idea of the fall carnival to the council. Pumpkins, carnival rides, and attractions to scare the faint of heart would bring in the locals. The attention of the mortals jumping with fear would entertain the Elite long enough to lure them into the festivities.

Abel would no doubt jump at the opportunity to bring the community together. Everyone knew it was an act that would bring him the praise for setting up the festival when he reported back to those who were higher up on the totem pole.

"What a marvelous idea, darling Aspyn,"

Ravana said. She had a hop in her step as I relayed the idea to her. It would make its way back to Abel in record time coming from the sinister angel's lips. I would be called upon soon enough.

"I am so glad you think so, Ravana," I said. A giddy feeling began to bubble in the pit of my stomach as I smiled at her. "As much as I would love to stay and discuss all the details, I do have to notes on my desk to file from the last meeting before Abel comes looking for them."

"Of course, you do." Ravana leaned in and placed two kisses in the air by my cheeks. "I knew I liked you for some reason."

Turning away from her, I couldn't help but let a devious smile settle across my face. Finley stood at the end of the corridor shaking his head at me.

"You are something else, Aspyn Faye." Finley laughed, wrapped an arm around my shoulders, and pulled me closer into him. "Did it work?"

"What do you think?" I looked up at him through my eyelashes.

"I think that you are being turned into my little devil, and I don't know if that is a good or bad thing." Finley's words tickled my ears as he nuzzled his nose into my hair. I shook my head at his statement.

"It's only a good thing for you," I said in a hushed tone. My hand slipped up to lace my fingers with his, and I pulled him toward the exit. "Come on, you know Asher will be dying to know how this went."

The new fall air nipped at my nose, causing me to scrunch it up at the sensation. This was my favorite time of year, and an event like a fall carnival would have had me jumping at the opportunity, but unfortunately this would be tarnished by the night's plans. 'Tis the season to be wicked, I suppose.

"He needs to learn some patience, I think." Finley's husky voice set my blood on fire. He tugged me in the direction of a shadowed corridor at the end of the square. The cobblestone buildings provided shelter from wandering eyes. My laugh echoed off the stones as Finley flipped me around, my body pressing up against their cool surface.

Finley draped his arms above me, forearms

trapping me within his grasp. He leaded down and kissed the side of my jaw. "You are so important to me, Aspyn."

My cheeks flushed a bright scarlet color as I let my forehead rest in the crook of his neck and breathed in his warm scent. Fin was home, and with him near, every part of me felt at peace. After all of this mess was over, the only constant I knew I could count on was Finley.

"Promise me one thing, Fin," I murmured, pulling myself away from him. I wanted to see his eyes when I asked him this. He stared at me with those wild blue eyes that I loved to get lost in. "Promise me that after everything is over, that we will be okay."

"Aspyn…" He hesitated.

I placed my hand against his cheek, stroking the soft skin with my thumb. He leaned into my touch like a magnet who needed its other half.

"I don't mean physically; hell, we could both be tortured and exiled like Mal was." My words came out in a breathy whisper. "What I mean is that we will be okay with whatever the other does.

No grudges or stupid arguments on what could have been done. Because I don't know if I could live with losing you."

Finley didn't respond with words; instead, he gripped onto the sides of my face and pulled me into a kiss. It felt desperate, like if he stopped for even one second, I would slip away in the wind that blew around us. He broke away from my lips sooner than I would have liked and placed his swollen lips to my forehead.

"I promise you this, Aspyn. That no matter what happens in the coming weeks, we will be all right. The thought of being away from you has never crossed my mind. We will get through this, darling."

Abel had fallen hard for the idea of a festival, just as we had predicted. I had been summoned to his personal chambers a day later.

My hand paused in the air as I went to knock on the wooden surface. I had never entered Abel's chambers, and they were a secret to the world that I never wanted to explore. I gulped down the dread and knocked softly on the door. The door swung open immediately by Abel's own ability to manipulate everything around him.

He sat behind a large black desk with gold hardware wrapping around itself to create intricate swirls on the piece's surface. Behind the man a fireplace was lit, flames burning so big that they almost jumped out of their contained space. The warmth flowed around the already heated room, causing a small bead of sweat to form at my hair line. My eyes caught sight of the paintings he had on the walls. They all told the story of how the Elite had come to inhabit earth.

One of them stood out to me. It was a huge painting which took up most of the left wall. Brilliant colors of red, black, and white shone against the canvas's glossy surface. The depiction of Lucifer falling from Heaven's gates was one I was familiar with. His beauty shone through even in painting, as long dark hair arched underneath itself in magnificent curls. The vibrant blue of his eyes stood out in the sea of angry red and black which floated around him.

I had only been privy to meet the angel once before his falling, and to say he was charming was an understatement. Asher had warned me of the destruction he was causing, which swayed me away from venturing back to speak with him.

"A beauty, is it not?" Abel said, his stare fixed on me with unwavering examination. "I find that this piece grounds us all to remember why we must do what we do to those who break our rules."

"Yes," I replied. "That is beautiful. Did you paint it yourself?"

"No." Abel chuckled. "I do believe that one was done by Tabitha Manson. She has a certain talent for creating the most wondrous art."

I turned to glance at the painting once more. The feeling of familiarity clung to me, and I couldn't shake it off. Taking one step closer to Abel, he beckoned me to sit in one of the two velvet chairs across from his desk. The purple material sank in as I settled down on it.

"You wished to speak with me?" I questioned, wanting this ensure meeting would be only as long as it had to be. Asher and Finley both tried hands.

"There is one more question I must ask you, Aspyn." Abel's tone stopped me in my tracks. Calmly I turned to look at his wicked smile. "There has been a rumor going around that Asher has been harboring the secret of where Alexander Caldwell is hiding."

I blinked once at him. "I am not sure what you are insinuating."

"Oh no, let me finish. The rumors continue to say that you both know the reason Rowen has seemingly abandoned her duties with the council. She has missed three callings. You wouldn't know anything about that, would you?"

Abel sat still, waiting for my answer. My face remained composed, but my mind was screaming to run. Run far away from the council and their rules until they could no longer pinpoint the location of the rogue angel.

"I have no idea what you are speaking about, Abel," I said, voice even and calm. Abel eyed me suspiciously, waiting to see a crack of deception shine through.

"You are well aware of the consequences if you were hiding what you are accused of from the council. I hope a smart girl such as yourself would know her worth to the Elite. We wouldn't want you to end up like the other demons in this town." Abel paused. "Would we?"

"No sir, we wouldn't."

Abel clapped his hands together, letting his feet fall from the desk as he sat straight once again. "Of course, we wouldn't. You are dismissed."

Chapter Fifteen
Before

Finley and Asher were waiting for my return outside of our home. One loose cigarette hung from Asher's fingertips, the smoke from it floating around the two of them, but he didn't bring it to lips once as I told them what Abel had said.

"So, there's a rat in our group." Asher tossed the cigarette on the step and smashed his foot into the surface. I ran my hand through my hair as my eyes wandered around to look at the other homes surrounding us. There weren't many, and most of them were abandoned. The only occupied one other than the Halloway's that I knew of was cattycorner to ours and was home to Gabriel Moreno. He wasn't much of a talker.

A light drizzle began to settle on my skin as I stared down the road. In the misty haze I could see a figure watching us from the darkness of the home's upstairs window. Chills crawled up my neck as a sway of a curtain began shadowing the figure from my sight, indicating that someone knew I had seen them.

"Come on." I motioned toward the front door. "There could be ears listening in."

The three of us made our way into the house, settling in the small kitchen in the back. I did the only thing I could think of doing and grabbed a baking sheet.

"What are you doing?" Asher gave me a wild look. I shrugged my shoulders before turning into the fridge and found the prepackaged sugar cookies. He rolled his eyes at me. "Unbelievable."

"I bake when I am stressed," I called over my shoulder at him.

"You were saying we have a rat in the group." Finley pulled Asher's attention away from the brewing argument. "Who could it be?"

"Normally I would accuse you out of habit,

but the look on your face when Aspyn informed us proved my suspicions wrong," Asher stated plainly. He plopped down at one of the chairs at the table.

Finley rolled his eyes at him and took the other chair for himself. "You always blame me first. Why is that?"

"You're an easy target, love," I said, sending him a wink when he glared at me. "Oh, come on, you are the highest ranked golden boy out of all of us. It just makes sense."

"Yeah, that and you were the tattle tale of the group when we were young," Asher said, dodging a shove from Finley. Placing a spoonful of raw dough in my mouth, I smiled at both of them. This was what I missed the most: the simple moments with the three of us. Where there was nothing but the risk of getting caught whispering in the back of a council meeting. Turning around, I let the oven's heat warm my face as I placed the cookie sheet in.

"Well, now that we have established it is none of us…" I walked around the countertop and lifted myself onto it to sit. "Who could it be?"

"My bets are on Ice Princess." Asher threw himself back into the chair to lean it back. The front two legs lifted from the ground, and it took all my willpower not to shove my foot against the back ones so he would topple over.

"It can't be Delaney; she has Mallory to worry about now." I rolled my eyes at Asher, who quirked an eyebrow at me. "Stop giving me that look. She wouldn't tell Tabby anything either. They are practically at each other's throats every time they are two feet from each other."

"Good point." Finley nodded, his eyebrows scrunched together in concentration. "What about—"

A knock on the front door rang out around us. I flicked my head toward the sound before hopping off the counter and starting toward it. Someone's hand caught my upper arm, pulling me back into the kitchen.

I turned to look at my twin. "What is your problem? It is probably someone one trying to sell us something or rope us into their New Age religion."

"In the rain?" Asher questioned. He nodded his head toward the window behind us. The water pelted down on the glass in violent droplets. I turned back toward the door where the persistent knocking was still happening.

"You don't think it's the coun—" I stopped mid-sentence to meet Asher's gaze. It was filled with an emotion between worry and anger. As if we both had the same thought, our bodies moved toward the back door. Yanking it open in a single swing, I sprinted out into the rain without bothering to wait for Asher. He would be right behind me.

"Are you two insane?" Finley screamed after us, his question only making me pick up speed. The wooden fence caging in the backyard was slick as I tried to scramble up the side barefoot. I could feel tiny pieces of wood stick into the palms of my hands as I pulled myself over the top. My foot slipped, causing me to topple headfirst into the ground below me.

I groaned in pain. The heavy stomp of boots landed next to my head, and I looked up to see Asher's laughing figure above me. Pushing myself upright, I glared at him. "Shut up if you know what's good for you, brother."

He hauled me to my feet. "I didn't say anything."

The sound of running made us both freeze. I prayed whoever it was had no intention of investigating over the fence. The side gate which sat to our left swung open, revealing a fully drenched Mallory.

"You two are the dumbest set of twins I have ever met," Mallory screamed over the rain. She turned to travel back through the fence's opening. "Come on, Xander wants an update on how the meeting went."

Chapter Sixteen
Before

The squish of the bottom of my jeans against the tile floor caught Finley's attention. He stifled a laugh as he examined the damage my brother and I brought upon ourselves.

"Why are you covered in mud?" A child sat at the kitchen table, his feet swinging back and forth as he sipped on a juice box. Nathaniel Caldwell was the spitting image of his father.

"Couldn't find a babysitter tonight, Xan?" Asher joked. He made his way to the table leaving small puddles as he went. Nate lit up at the sight of my brother. Asher reached out and ruffled Nate's hair. "Hey little man, staying out of trouble I hope?"

Nathaniel smiled a large toothy grin. "I got a

green light today in school."

"The first in weeks," Xander grumbled. "Nate, go with Delaney. She said she had a surprise to give you for your good behavior today."

At the mention of a surprise, Nate's entire face lit up like a freshly decorated Christmas tree. He jumped from his chair and began to race out of the room but paused and turned in my direction. Scrunching my eyebrows together, I didn't understand why he was staring at me.

"Nate, come on." Delaney stood just outside of the hallway, her hand outstretched for him. Nate ignored her and craned his neck to look up at my towering figure.

"Miss Claire told me that you like riddles." Nate blinked once at me. I sputtered to respond but he was too impatient to wait for me to answer. "She said to ask you one."

I quirked up my eyebrow at him. "Okay, let's hear it."

"What gets harder to destroy the older I get?"

"I don't know, Nathaniel." I leaned down to get eye level with him. "What's the answer?"

Nate shrugged his shoulders. "The Night Monster."

He turned around and walked back to Delaney, who just ushered him out of the room quickly. She turned to look over her shoulder at us, a worried look plastered across her face. The blood in my veins ran cold; something about that name felt like a warning.

"Asp?" Finley ran a soothing hand down my arm. "You're shaking. Are you okay, darling?"

I nodded numbly. "Just cold."

"Why don't you go up and get changed out of those wet clothes? Asher and Finley will fill me in on your meeting with Abel," Xander said. His voice felt distant to me.

"Okay," I mumbled, before disappearing into the darkness of the hallway.

Chapter Seventeen
Before

When I was finished changing into dry clothes, I made my way quietly down the stairs. The voices of the three men in the kitchen floated around the silent home. I halted at the edge of the last step, listening to them speak.

"What is going on with her?" Xander's voice sounded tired, and I could almost see him running one hand over his face in attempt to hide his exhaustion.

"Aspyn?" Asher questioned. "It seemed that whatever your son said about a night monster set her on edge tonight."

"Nathaniel said Claire told him to tell her that riddle. Do you think he is telling the truth?"

Finley's voice was muffled by the sound of a chair being pulled across the floor.

"Claire? No, I bet he heard it from one of the children at school and thought it would be funny to mess with an adult," Xander snapped. "He's been acting out these past few months."

I shifted my weight to one foot, causing the bottom step to let out a squeak. The sound gave away my hiding spot, and seconds later Finley peered around the corner of the hallway. A warm smile spread across his face when he saw me.

"Hey," Finley said softly. He reached out a hand, beckoning me to come closer. "We were just finishing up telling Xander about the meeting."

I smiled sadly at him before taking his hand in mine. We didn't move for a moment, just stood in each other's presence. Finley leaned down and placed a kiss on my temple.

"You okay?" he mumbled into the kiss.

"Yeah, it's just been a long day, that's all," I said. Turning my head, I moved back to see him. His eyes were examining me with the precision he had when trying to solve a puzzle that was broken apart. But I wasn't a game that need to be put back together.

"Are you two done yet?" Asher asked in the same bored tone he always gave us when we were caught up in each other around him.

I rolled my eyes before pushing around Fin. "Don't worry, Ash. You will always be my favorite."

Plopping down in the chair next to him, I sent him a playful smile. He shoved his shoulder into mine lightly, and I actually laughed a real laugh for once in a long while. It felt good to be happy even if it was just for a moment.

"Aspyn," Xander called. I turned my attention to him and noticed the cookie he had hanging loosely toward me.

I gasped. "Well, I'm glad someone remembered those because we wouldn't be sitting in this kitchen if they hadn't."

"You're welcome," Finley said. He stood in the same spot of the kitchen I had left him in. Back leaning against the doorway as he continued to watch me.

Xander continue to dangle the cookie out in front of me. "If you don't eat it, I will."

I snatched the treat from his hand, the warmth from the oven still clinging to the bottom. "So, I assume these two filled you in on what Abel requested."

"Yes." Xander rounded the countertop, stopping right in front of me, and leaned back against the edge. "And you are going to give him everything he wants plus more. Make this carnival the most brilliant spectacle Idelwood has ever seen."

"What's the underlying plan you have cooked up?" I asked, picking the crystalized sugar off the cookie. Suddenly the thought of eating the sugary treat made my stomach roll. Everyone in the room was watching me closely, like if they said the wrong thing, I would lose my mind. Not that they didn't have reason to believe this.

I made eye contact with Asher. He ran a hand over his jaw slowly. "Rowen and Claire are leaving the night of the festival. With everyone distracted, there will be a smaller chance of them getting caught."

"Okay." I nodded. "And all I have to do is be a distraction by throwing a carnival so good that even the Elite can't help but be enamored with it?"

"Well..." Fin scratched the back of his head awkwardly.

"We also need your help getting Claire to Rowen during the festival," Xander clarified. He crossed his arms over his chest, waiting for my challenge.

"Does she have to make an appearance? Say she caught the flu or something that makes it so she can be away without drawing any attention to herself?"

"If the Halloways' only child doesn't show up to an important town event, that will draw suspicion from not only the Elite but the locals as well. When has Claire not been present at a town event?" Asher quirked an eyebrow up at me. He had a point; the Halloway family was the image of perfection in the town of Idelwood. Being that Claire's father was the preacher, everyone looked to him as if he were placed on a pedestal. In reality, Abel had offered him the job when the last one had mysteriously vanished.

"What if something goes terribly wrong?" I whispered. The pressure of having lives in my hands was beginning to weigh heavily on me. If I messed this up, it affected all of us in one way or another. Looking up, I met Asher's sad eyes. "I don't want to be the one you blame forever if this ends badly."

"Rowen will get out either way. There is no question of that." Asher's voice shook slightly, giving away the lie he was trying to tell me. "Your only job is to try to get Claire to her. If it doesn't work, we will send Mallory with her."

"And if I get caught, I will fall for this."

Finley stood upright from his slouched position. "We'll all fall for this if it come to that."

"Through hell and back," I whispered with a sad smile that matched the others in the room.

Chapter Eighteen
Before

The scent of candied apples reminded me of my first date with Finley. We had attended a carnival hosted by the local high school. It was the same school the council tried make us attend, but their pleas were lackluster. The two of us had climbed the fire escape of the school's roof with a brown paper bag clenched between my front teeth. I made my way to the edge of the roof where we could see the entire town in all of its glittering glory.

Inhaling deeply the scent of melting caramel, I begged to be back on that rooftop with sticky fingers and a redheaded boy whose smile shone brighter than the fireworks filling the night air.

"Do you need help?" A voice snapped me out of my trance. I turned around, meeting the gaze of Claire Halloway who was holding a box of what looked to be fake blood and bats for the haunted maze.

My hand gripped the orange and black streamers I had been twisting around one another. They crunched together in a crumbled mess and I sighed, throwing the ruined pieces down and picking up the rolls of paper once again. "No, I think I am good here, Claire."

Claire huffed out an angry breath in my direction before turning toward the large rows of corn that had been shaped into the horrifying maze. She made it only a few steps before spinning back around to me and throwing down the box. A bottle of fake blood exploded on impact. It splattered up Claire's white T-shirt, but she didn't seem to mind or notice the dark liquid.

"You're not the only one who has something to lose, Aspyn." Claire's harsh words cut across the space between us. My eyes widened in astonishment. She had never spoken with such force before to any of us. I sputtered to find the right words, but she held up a hand to silence me. "Some of us just found what they have always known was out there, and it threatens to be destroyed."

"Claire, you don't think I don't understand that you are risking everything to help them. You are going to lose your home, your fath—"

Claire's sadistic laugh cut through my words. "My father? I couldn't care less about him. And I was never in love with this town."

I shook my head. "Then what else could be left here? We will still be around, I promise."

Taking a step forward, I reached out to grab the girl's hand, but she ripped it away from my touch. Claire's eyes weren't trained on mine anymore, their dark color filling with a mix of anger and sadness as she stared beyond my head.

"Just be grateful you have Finley; some of us aren't so lucky to be in love with a person we can spend the rest of our mortal lives with."

Claire twisted back to the box behind her, picking items and dashing off into the maze without another word to me. I craned my neck behind me to see what she had been so enamored with. A soft gasp left my parted lips as I watched Gabe stare at the spot where Claire had just gone to hide.

His gaze flicked over to mine, a deep scowl settling on his face. Gabe stepped back into the shadows the setting sun had brought on, disappearing like a predator into the woods.

Chapter Nineteen
Before

Screams of delighted terror filled the night air. I stepped out of the town hall, checking off the last-minute touches that had to be completed before I could enjoy what was left of my time. A child in a vampire costume chased a young princess around the angel statue in front of me. The little girl shrieked out giggles as the vampire boy caught her, pretending to suck her blood in a dramatic fashion.

I smiled lightly at their childlike innocence. A soft brush of a hand touched my upper arm, causing the smile to grow wider on my face. Twisting around, I launched my body into Finley's. He caught me effortlessly and nuzzled his face into the crook of my neck.

"I like that reaction." Finley's hot breath tickled my collar bone.

I pulled back to look at him. "I missed you."

"And that has nothing to do with what is happening tonight?"

My shoulders dropped at the reminder. I gulped down my fear. "Can we not talk about it?"

Finley watched me, his blue eyes waiting for me to crack. But I couldn't think about Claire, Rowen, or the baby that would soon be here. Running one hand over his jawline, "Of course. Come on, I want to show you something while I have your undivided attention."

His hand gripped mine, guiding me to the edge of the carnival. The sound of popcorn popping in a random vendors tent floated around us as he continued through a small opening in the corn maze.

"Where are we going?" I laughed as the cornstalks caught my hair.

Even in the dark I could make out the ghostly smirk pulling at Finley's lips. "You have never been able to wait for the surprise, have you?"

"Not when the surprise involves a guy dragging me through a dark corn maze," I said, laughing as he threw me an annoyed look over his shoulder. "You could kill me out here and no one would even know."

"Or I could do this." Finley stopped mid-step and crashed his lips to mine. I smiled into the kiss and pulled at the sides of the worn jean jacket he had on. His hand dropped to my hips, pulling me flush to his body. Reaching up, I tugged at the baby hairs at the nape of his neck, causing him to moan into the kiss.

"I am going to gouge my eyes later tonight." Asher's voice pulled us back to reality. I felt my entire face flame up in embarrassment. Mallory stood next to him, hand across her mouth in a silent laugh.

"I'll help." Mallory shoved her shoulder into his. She stepped forward, holding out a phone to me. "Xander said he will call you on this when it is time. It's a burner phone—that way the council will have no idea you had anything to do with

Rowen's disappearance."

I took the phone in my hands and pocketed it in the back of my jeans. We were all silent for a moment, the sounds of the distant carnival filling the empty space. The corn rustled beside Asher, and I snapped my attention toward the motion. A figure stood in the shadows. It was tall with piercing eyes that were watching all of us with hawk-like precision. Nudging Finley, I motioned toward the figure, but everyone was already staring at them.

Slowly the figure emerged from its hiding space, revealing Gabe. He walked with confidence as if he knew every secret we held on to. I could only assume whatever of love affair was happening with Claire, gave him insight into our group. Asher nodded at him, waiting for Gabe to speak first, but he stayed silent.

"Gabe." It was Mallory who spoke first. "It's great to see you."

Mal bounced on the balls of her feet with nervous energy. This was one of the first people she had seen outside of the group since she had fallen. Most of the Elite were prejudiced against the fallen and I could see the fear written across her face. Gabe had never been one to take kindly to the fallen. Tension rolled off his broad shoulders as he watched the Manson girl.

"Hello, Mallory." Gabe nodded stiffly, trying his best to be cordial. He turned toward me. "What is the plan for tonight?"

Startled by the boldness of his statement, I took a step back into Finley. He gripped down on the belt loop of my dark jeans and pulled me closer to his chest. We had been caught, but in a way, I felt more terrified that it was by Gabe. He could run back to the council the second he was out of our sight, and we had no control over what would occur then.

"I have the festival's schedule," I sputtered out. My hand dug into the inside pocket of my leather jacket to find the crumpled piece of paper that had the tentative schedule I had scrawled out.

Gabe held up his hand, stopping my frantic movements. "Cut the theatrics, Aspyn. We both know that Claire slipped up."

Asher flicked his eyes toward me. They burned

with anger at the unknown mistake that was being exposed. I sucked in a deep breath. "I had my suspicions about the two of you, but I was not positive."

"Claire?" Finley hissed. He started around me in angry strides. I leaped into his path, placing both hands on his chest and gave him a light shove to stop him from attacking Gabe. Fin glared at me. "What is going on, Aspyn?"

"It's not what you think, Fin," I whispered. "Claire and Gabe…"

My voice trailed off; truly I did not know what to label the relationship between the two of them. I looked to Gabe for the answers.

"I am in love with Claire," Gabe said with conviction. There was no questioning those words. They were strong, and you could feel the emotion he had for the girl course through them.

Finley stepped back in astonishment. "But didn't your ceremony say that Ta—"

"It doesn't matter what that water trick said," Gabe growled. "The person who appeared in the water and I both agreed that it was better if we remained just as acquaintances."

Mallory flinched inwardly. "You know that statement only comes from one person in the situation."

I had not been at Gabe's ceremony, as I was pulled away to gather the folder that condemned Xander for his crimes. The whole thing was never a second thought to me after the news. Now I tried to rack my brain for who had been matched with Gabe, but no one came to mind.

Shaking my head, I tried to veer back to the conversation's main point. "Why are you two not surprised with this revelation?"

Asher and Mallory stared back at me. They were unfazed about Claire and Gabe, which could only mean they knew about their relationship before today. Asher narrowed his eyes. "Claire informed us about them when it was deemed to be of importance, little sister."

I scoffed at him, letting my mind wander as Asher explained to Gabe what the plan was for tonight. Gabe's eyes kept flicking toward me as my brother spoke.

"Are you sure you are up for this, Aspyn?" Gabe asked, his eyes pleading for the correct answer. My heart tightened for the angel who was in love with the mortal girl. I went to open my mouth to assure him that I could do this when the shrill tone of a phone ringing cut me off. Asher reached in his jean pocket, digging out the device before flipping it open and placing it against his ear.

"Xander?" Asher's face fell at the response on the other end. "What?"

I stepped closer to my twin, trying to hear the muffled voice on the other end of the call. But it was no use as Asher had the phone pressed so close to his ear that barely any sound was coming from the speaker.

"Are we to continue as planned?" Asher's voice was frantic. "Okay. I will inform her."

He let the phone fall limply to his side, eyes glazed over with a far-off look. "Rowen had the baby. We need to find Claire now

Chapter Twenty
Before

Flashing lights from the spinning Ferris wheel illuminated Asher's face as he ran through plan B. I was to find Claire, who I had assigned to work in the haunted corn maze. At the time, her being hidden in miles of darkness was the perfect way to get her out of town without anyone noticing. Now, it had turned into our worst nightmare.

"Asher," I panted, trying to keep up with his long strides.

Asher halted mid-step, and I ran directly into his back. He turned around, facing me before looking just beyond my head at the other three trailing behind us. I twisted around to look over my shoulder. Mallory had pulled her black hood over her pale hair to hide her face. Even in the darkness that hid her features, the gray of her vibrant eyes stood out like two glowing lights. Finley watched me, concern lacing his features while Gabe stood stoic as ever.

"We need to find her, Asp," Asher said in a low whisper. Turning my gaze back on him, I knew there was no other option. His eyes flitted around like a wild animal searching for a predator. "Mal, council members to your right. Get out of here now."

Mallory's glowing eyes flicked over to the ring toss that Abel and Ravana stood at. The sneaky angel ran her fingertips up his arm, laughing at some awful joke he told, no doubt. I rolled my eyes at them before looking back at the now-empty spot Mallory had just stood in.

"I'll try her cell one more time," Gabe grumbled. He stepped away us as he lifted his phone to his ear.

"I need to go," Asher said in a hushed tone. He started toward the townhall, but I caught his arm and pulled him back to me.

"What are you going to do?" I whispered, my voice shaking with fear.

"I just have to do this one thing, and then I will meet you back at the cabin with Claire. It is better if neither of you have any knowledge of what I am about to do."

I stared at my twin, waiting for him to give me any type of hint that I could hold onto, but he didn't budge. Launching my body into his arms, I squeezed my brother with all the might I could muster. He returned the favor with a light touch.

"I love you, Asher. Please be careful," I whimpered into his neck. Hot tears streaked down my face as I let go and watched him fade into the multicolored carnival haze. The crowd of locals swallowed his figure, leaving me standing in the middle of the busy walkway.

"Come on, Asp." Finley tugged my arm in the direction of the corn maze. I was numb—everything in me knew if Asher got caught, he would be lost to me.

The screams of terror echoed in the night air as Finley and I both stood at the entrance of the maze.

Emaline Chadwick and William Goodwin sat at a fold-out table taking tickets from those wanting to experience a slight scare for the night.

"Finley," William called from the table. I shoved Fin slightly in his direction as William made his way around the table. Finley took the outstretched hand in his own, giving it a firm shake. "How have you been? The guys have missed you at the last few meetings."

Finley let out a loud laugh. "Oh, you know how it is."

I could feel his eyes look over to me, insinuating that we just couldn't leave each other's side for more than ten seconds. Rolling my eyes, I crossed my arms over my chest, trying to brace myself from the cold glare that was coming from Emaline. She was trying to not be obvious with her looks, but they were burning a hole in the side of my skull.

"I could use some help getting the refills of ice buckets over to the snow cone stand." William jutted his thumb toward Cee's café where we were storing the extra food for the carnival. "Can you spare a few moments away from your girl to help an old friend out?"

Finley peered over toward me. "Let me ask Aspyn."

Quickly he made his way back to me. "I can tell him no."

"Keep both of them distracted," I mumbled, my eyes wandering back to Emaline's accusing ones. "Emaline looks like she is about to snitch me out to the entire council. If you are around, it will keep her from wandering into things that don't concern her."

Finley's hand cupped the underside of my chin, guiding my face up to his. This kiss felt different from any other one we had previously shared. It was filled with sadness, as if by just this one simple gesture we both acknowledged this night was not going to end well. I pulled away, knowing we didn't have time to dwell in each other's company. I needed to find Claire, and he needed to be as far away from the situation as I could place him.

"Be safe," Finley said against my cheek before walking back to William.

I turned to the entrance of the maze and let the

darkness of the night swallow me whole.

Wind howled through the shifting corn as I ventured deeper into it. Local teens squealed and ran past me as a masked figure chased after them with a flimsy blood-covered Halloween knife. The watery blood swayed haphazardly through the plastic of the toy, making the entire gimmick look like a horrible knock-off version of *Scream*.

I darted left into a long row that Mal had told me to follow when I came looking for Claire. The crunch of leaves behind me caused me to whip around to see who could be following me. But there was no one standing anywhere in sight.

"If you are trying to scare me, it's not going to work," I growled. "I set up this entire thing, so if you want to get paid tonight, I suggest you move along to another girl wandering through these parts."

Silence. I sighed loudly. My boots crunched against the dirt, leaving whatever local kid who thought he got the scare of night in the bag alone. The rustling sounded again only a few feet down the row. Black hair wrapped itself around the corn stalks as a girl raced through them. Her nightgown was so white it glowed in the moonlight.

"Hey," I called after the girl. My feet carried me forward and off the path of the maze. The wisps of hair disappeared into the darkness, but I could still hear her soft giggles as she tore through the path. I dug the tips of my fingers down my face in frustration. She was just one of the local kids who wanted to scare me, but something inside me was curious why she had lured me out of the maze and onto this path if that was her goal.

"Don't lead the guests out of the corn. I don't need to lose anyone in the maze tonight."

It was the one rule I had reiterated a hundred times to the actors. Shrugging off the nerves, I didn't have time for them right now. Not if I wanted to get to Claire in time. I turned to head back to the maze, but the corn all looked the same to me. There was no glow of the soft lantern light we use to illuminate the paths that could lead me back. Whipping around in a tight circle, I tried to remember the exact steps I had just taken. Another soft giggle floated through the wind. The sound felt so close I could feel the girl's hot breath on the back of my neck.

"Okay, this isn't funny anymore," I shouted out into the open air. "You have had your fun. Now show me back into the maze."

I paused, waiting for the sound once again, but nothing came. Reaching into my jacket, I dug out my cellphone to try and get Finely to come find me. The phone let out a low-pitched sound, indicating the phone was dying and fast. In the left corner of the screen, the service bar was at nothing. I groaned at the thing, holding it above my head, and began to walk forward to gain even one bar of service.

"Come on, come on," I whispered to the device. The moment it gained service, an earsplitting scream shot through the night air. I jumped, throwing the phone in the process, and listened as the screaming continued. It wasn't the same as the ones that had been spilling through the corn all night from frightened guests. No, this one matched a certain mortal girl I was supposed to be protecting.

Claire Halloway's screams continued to ring in my ears as I dropped down to snatch up my cellphone. I stumbled through the corn, trying to find my way to the girl, but every path I took looked the same and without the trail guiding me, there was no telling where in the maze I had ended up.

Bursting through the corn, I landed upon a dead-end trail. It was dark in this corner, and the eerie silence of Claire's screams sent a chill down my spine. I cautiously wandered up the pathway, looking for anyone who might know where the exit was. As I came into a four-way break in the corn, a boy with a pig mask pushed up onto his hair sprinted through the middle path.

"Hey," I called out to him, but he flew past me as if he hadn't even seen me. Following in the direction he had just come, I tried to see what had spooked him so much that he would rush away from me.

I smelled the smoke before I saw the flames.

Chapter Twenty-One
Before

An angry fire was burning its way through the corn. Turning around, I dashed away from the flames, but they followed me like hot breath on my back. Large pieces of ash rained down on me, leaving dark soot scorching my body. I gasped out in pain as the fire began to lick the bottoms of my feet. Its burning tongue caught my calf and sent me flying forward onto the ground.

Scrambling onto my hands and feet, I tried to push away from the fire. The movement felt like when you would play cat as a child in a clumsy fashion. Finally getting to my feet, I kept moving toward the nearest exit. Over my shoulder, the flames swirled in a synchronized dance. They were beautiful in the most destructive way imaginable.

I threw myself through another row of corn, this time finding the forest which led up to the church right in front of me. Turning around, I looked up at the flames, but they had stopped coming at me. They were just floating in place like an invisible wall was extinguishing them into a giant billow of angry smoke. I exhaled through my nose as I watched the last plume of smoke disappeared.

The front of the church was dark. A single light swung off its bolt in the wind. The fixture was ripped from the wall, but the structure was still holding onto it by its wires. I moved closer, the energy around the church became darker with every step. The harsh stench of burnt wood filled my nostrils. I could see the remnants of smoke coming off a pew where the fire had been extinguished.

There was blood smeared across the normally pristine walls in long streaks as if someone was running a hand across them. The pews and altar table were thrown across the room in giant piles of splintered wood. But what horrified me the most was the hanging noose that swung ominously in the front of the church.

I turned to run from the gruesome scene, but the light cries of a baby broke through the church's walls and stopped me in my tracks. Twisting back to the altar hall, I followed the sound to the single pew that sat upright in the front of the room. I rounded the corner, coming upon a newborn baby swaddled in a purple blanket. The corner had the child's named embroidered on it. Liliana Caldwell was lying right in front of me, the child who was to be the damnation of us all. I leaned down and cradled her close to my chest as I tried to shush her cries.

"Claire," I called out. My voice shook, but no one called back to me. Not that I had expected them to; I could figure out what had occurred in this space without saying it out loud.

Stepping over the wreckage, I made my way back outside with the baby clutched in one arm and my phone pressed to the opposite ear. I tried Xander first, but it went directly to voice mail. Same thing happened with Asher and everyone else in the group. Then I dialed the last number I thought would be helpful.

"Did you find her?" Gabe's husky voice spoke through the other end of the line. I could tell that underneath the masked voice he was freaking out.

"No," I said, voice cracking as the tears began to flow down my face. "I am not sure what happened, but her father's church is destroyed, and I found something that shouldn't have been left behind in the destruction."

"The child?" Gabe's voice shook with emotion.

I answered with a sob and pulled Liliana closer to me. She was peacefully asleep in my arms, the light fuzz of red hair that matched her mother's peeking through the knit hat she wore.

"What do I do now, Gabe? No one is answering, and I can't very well waltz through the town square with Liliana in my arms."

"Claire said the group had a cabin the council was unaware of."

"Yes." I nodded even if he could not see my motion.

"Go there. I'll find your brother and Finley.

We'll meet you there once we know it is safe to do so," Gabe said, voice confident that we could pull this off.

"Okay. Stay safe." I whispered.

The line went dead without a goodbye. The sting of the burns had finally appeared and every time the wind brushed past one, the wound burned even hotter. I hissed at the pain as I trudged over the bridge. The cabin was a good distance from the church, and I didn't want to get caught in the storm I could smell was coming in.

"Well, what do we have here?" A menacing voice called out.

I froze, fear coursing through my veins as I turned to make eye contact with Abel, Ravana, and Emaline Chadwick. Abel stood, arms crossed over his chest, while Ravana hung off him like a cheap date he couldn't shake. Emma was off to the side, hands wringing together in a nervous movement. She couldn't make eye contact with me. They stood on the other side of the bridge, staring at the child bundled up in my arms.

"Abel," I said. "I was coming to check in

on Claire. She spoke to me over the phone and informed me they need more supplies for the haunted maze, but when I arrived the entire church was destroyed. This child was left in the middle of the wreckage."

I gestured toward the baby, who stirred slightly and let out a quiet whimper. Abel moved a step closer trying to get a better look at Liliana, but I shifted backward and out of his view.

"Is that so?" Abel questioned, peering over his glasses to examine my lie. "Too bad your band of misfits was already apprehended, and we know all about this pathetic excuse for a plan to assist the Caldwell's."

"Yes, that abomination in your arms can't be allowed to leave," Ravana hissed at me. "She threatens the Elites with the demon blood that runs through her."

I laughed. "You and I both know that the fallen are no more demons than you are."

"Even so," Abel said reaching out a hand, "the child must be handled by the council. She will be evaluated to see if she is fit to be in this world."

"Liliana is just a baby," I whispered, staring at each of them with horror.

"It is for the best," Emaline's timid voice called to me. I stared at the girl for a moment, waiting for her to make eye contact with me to see that she did not know what she was speaking of.

"Give me the child now, Aspyn, or I will have your wings ripped out of your spine tonight," Abel shouted, causing me to look back at him. Fire shone in his eyes, and I knew he had no intention of letting me keep my wings even if I handed over the child.

Gulping down the lump in the back of my throat, I glanced down at Liliana's sleeping form once more. I couldn't hand her over to the evil that bred in the council. That was not something I would allow her to grow up in. She deserved to thrive around people who adored her, someone who was excited for her first steps and would record them for her to watch over again when she was older. No, Liliana did not deserve to be poked and prodded just because an angel fell in love with a demon.

Spinning on my heel, I raced away from Abel's shouting figure. I did not care if I lost my wings for this, at least I'd lose them fighting for someone who could not fight for herself. Bursting into the entryway of the church, I ran toward Claire's father's private study. The door was unlocked, and inside nothing had been disturbed by the altercation that had occurred just outside. I slammed the door shut and locked it in place. Searching around, I tried to find somewhere to hide Liliana. In the corner of the room a shaking figure was huddled against the wall.

"Nathaniel?" I whispered. He snapped his head up to meet my eyes. The same blue eyes that he shared with his father were filled with tears. "Hey, what are you doing in here?"

"Claire told me to hide here and not come out until she came back," Nathaniel whimpered out the last part.

I crouched down to get level with him. "But she never came back, did she?"

"No." He shook his head before cowering back into himself.

Looking back at the locked door, I weighed my options. One: we all got caught like sitting ducks in here and both children were taken in by the council. Two: I gave Liliana to Nathaniel and told him to run to the first town that he saw. The doors handle began to rattle as someone tried to enter the room.

"Okay, come on." I reached out a hand, which he gladly took. Pulling him along, I made my way over to the open window behind the desk that sat in the middle of the room. "I am going to jump out of the room, but you have to hold Lily. Can you do that for me?"

Nathaniel nodded. He held his hands out for me to place his sister in. After she settled in his grip, I threw both legs out the window and shimmied my way down to the ground. The drop wasn't far, but I was trying to make the least amount of noise possible.

"Hand me her." I reached up for Liliana, who Nathaniel happily handed to me. "Can you jump out by yourself?"

The boy looked at me, his father's famous

smirk plastered across his face. "I could do this sleepwalking."

I silently laughed at him, waiting patiently as he snuck out the window and landed softly next to me. Breathing in one shaky breath, I got back down to his level. "Now, you have to take Liliana and run. Go to the next town over, and tell them your parents are gone. That you have nowhere to go, and someone will help you."

"Lily." Nathaniel locked eyes with me, "I like when you called her Lily."

I smiled at him, brushing back a stray lock of dark hair from his face. "Lily it is then."

"Will you come find us?" he asked hopefully.

"I'm not sure, buddy," I said softly. There was a commotion coming from the door of the office once again, and I thrust Liliana's tiny body into her brother's arms. "Go now."

Nathaniel must have heard the panic in my voice because without hesitation he rushed into the forest behind me. I watched the boy disappeared into the darkness hoping he was smart enough to navigate them to the nearest town.

"Why did you do that?" said Emaline's soft voice called out just to my right. I turned to look at her. She had betrayed her best friend and was ready to sell Rowen's children to the council as science experiments.

"It was the right thing to do," I said, standing up straight before dusting off the dirt that had collected on my pants. "Are you going to rat me out to Abel now?"

"No," she said sternly. My eyes traveled down to a cream envelope in her hand. Xander's handwriting was scrawled across it in his distinct loopy way. Emma noticed my gaze, slowly pulling the letter out of my sight. "I didn't know Abel had thoughts of killing the child if he deemed her a danger. I would never do that to Rowen."

I scoffed at her and started in the direction of town square, but her voice called back to me, "I'll keep what I heard a secret, but you do know she will find her way back here one day. Right?"

"Let's just hope when that occurs, she can hold her own against the Elites," I said, matching the smirk tugging at her lips.

"Oh, I have no doubt she'll be able to. With those parents of hers, she will bend every rule that Abel has set forth, and I cannot wait to see her in all her glory."

Chapter Twenty-Two
Before

Empty popcorn containers rolled across the cobblestone pathway in town. The carnival's activities were long gone, but the ghostly music that had been playing earlier still floated lightly around the square. Looking at the only home I had ever known, I didn't recognize it. The rose-colored glasses I had once viewed Idelwood with were removed, and now I was left with the vile scum that coated every inch of this town.

"Every Elite member is looking for you." Finley's gruff voice broke me from my trance. He stood just in front of me, hands casually in his pockets. There was a playful smile on his face.

"I know." I looked away from him. The next

words about to come out of my mouth would break him, and I couldn't witness his face when I said them. "I'm turning myself over to the council."

"What?" Finley's voice rose an octave. He stepped forward to close the space between us, which I matched with one of my own backward. My gaze traveled up to meet his hurt-filled eyes for the first time. "We could leave, just get in the car and drive to anywhere but here."

"I can't do that you, Fin," I growled at him, the anger of everything that had occurred bubbling to the surface. "I don't want to go anywhere with you."

I stepped around him, but Finley caught my arm and pulled me back to him. "If this is about Asher, then you should know something."

"What?" I kept my eyes trained in front of me.

"He sold Claire out," Finley whispered. The words made me snap my head toward him. Fin was looking down at the ground, regret racking his entire body.

"He wouldn't do that," I scoffed, trying to rationalize the idea in my head. "Claire was

Liliana's only way out of Idelwood. He wouldn't risk that."

Finley's eyes met mine. "Abel told him if he revealed where Claire and the child were, then he'd spare you the loss of your wings."

I shook my head. "No. Asher wouldn't take that deal."

Sinking into Finley's grip, I watched his face grow a shade paler. "Would he?"

Finley's silence was all the confirmation that was needed. I pulled myself from his grip, running my hands through my hair as I went round and round with Asher's decision.

"It doesn't matter," I finally said after a long moment of silence. "Abel caught me with Liliana, and I sent her off with Nathaniel, so my fate is sealed."

"It doesn't have to be." Finley traced the back of his hand against my cheek.

I pulled away from his touch and began down the path once again. "If I don't do this, Finley, then I will always feel guilty for Claire."

"Aspyn!" Finley hollered after me, but I

continued down the path. I refused to turn around to meet his stare. Warm tears streaked down my face as he spoke. "You don't have to condemn yourself for what Asher has done. He doesn't have to take you down with him."

"Of course, he does," I whispered, venom coating my words as I marched to meet my maker.

EPILOGUE
AFTER

Fresh snow powdered the clearing's cliff. I stood in the clouds watching them shift around me in dazzling shapes, but none of them made the pain in my chest lighten. The feeling of having my wings ripped from my back didn't even touch the heartbreak that was coursing through my entire body. It felt like someone was driving a hammer against my soul every second of the day.

"You came," I said as the person I requested to meet with arrived.

"Did you doubt I would?" Finley's voice was hard. I didn't expect him to be cheerful, but the coldness in his voice slammed another layer of hurt into my heart. Turning around, I met the eyes of the boy I still loved but could no longer have. His eyebrows scrunched together as he examined me.

"Your eyes." Finley motioned when he finally had the courage to meet them.

My hand flew up to trace my lash line. "Oh, yeah. It's a side effect of falling."

"I know," Finley sneered at me.

"Right. Xander." I scratched the back of my head. "Look, I asked you to come here to inform you that you don't have to worry about me. I am going to disappear out of your life."

He laughed darkly. "Is that what you think I want, Aspyn?"

"I don't want to ruin your life any more than I already have. It's better this way."

"For whom?" Finley shouted, his voice bouncing off the clearing floor and echoing through the trees. "For you? Because you made a decision that not only affected you but me as well. One that you did not think to ask my opinion on. Or for Asher? Whom I assume is leading your gang of misfits now."

I stood there shocked at his outburst. The hair on the back of my neck stood up from his words. Shaking my head, I refused to cry in front of him.

"We promised each other, Asp." Finley's words were laced with hurt, and I could see even from yards away his eyes were shining with fresh tears.

"I know," I whispered, "And I broke that promise, which I am sorry for, but I can't see you anymore."

"Just tell me you are doing this because you believe it will protect me."

I gulped back the bile that was rising out of my throat. This moment was one I had rehearsed countless times in the mirror, but the feeling that was bubbling up made me want to crumble to dust. There was only one way to get him to realize that he needed to move on and become the Elite member he was destined to be. It was better this way.

"I don't love you anymore, Fin," I hissed out, my words cold as ice. His face shattered for a moment before composing back to a haunted version of him.

"Well, it seems that there is nothing else to say," Finley said through a clenched his jaw. "Even if it is a lie."

I met his eyes once more, my lips moving to fix my mistake. Fin. I had called him Fin, not Finley. He turned on his heel, disappearing down the snow-covered mountain. When his figure was out of sight, I sank down on my knees and let the snow soak into my jeans. A strangled sob broke through my lips as Asher emerged from the tree line he had been hiding in.

"I'm sorry, Aspyn," he said roughly. I turned to look at where he stood off to the side to keep his distance. My temper had been unpredictable when he was around me as of late, and I couldn't control my new power just yet.

"Why did you sell her out?" I choked out the words. Asher's face dropped in regret. He reached up, running a hand over the light stubble that he hadn't bothered to shave.

"I thought I was saving you," Asher mumbled. He began his descent down the trail. I watched him grow smaller as he went, my mind whirling around the sacrifices we had all made this past year. And the ones we would give when the Night Monster returned.

My, My What Has Gotten Into My Little Devil

Claire Halloway
&
Gabe Moreno

The Reapers Symphony

He was a monster. But not the typical one who lurked in your closet at night. No, this monster was beautiful, and when he looked at me, I saw the good that begged to be seen. And oh, how I pleaded for it to reveal itself.

PLAYLIST

FIND THE FULL PLAYLIST & MORE ON SPOTIFY:
AUTHORALLISONALDRIDGE

STONE
JAYMES YOUNG

ILLICIT AFFAIRS
TAYLOR SWIFT

THE LOUVRE
LORDE

YOU
KEATON HENSON

DANCING WITH YOUR GHOST
SASHA ALEX SLOAN

HOME
CATIE TURNER

CALLS ME HOME
SHANNON LABRIE

IN CASE YOU DON'T LIVE FOREVER
BEN PLATT

SEE YOU LATER (TEN YEARS)
JENNA RAINE

Chapter One
Claire Halloway

As if my life couldn't get any worse in this cursed town, I was stuck volunteering at the church's annual bake sale. Don't get me wrong, I loved a good baked good as much as the rest of the residents in this town, but I had long-standing plans that I did not want to break.

My father did not care for excuses, and so here I stood, the fakest smile I could conjure upon my face as I handed the little old lady who sat in the second row at every Sunday service a chocolate chip cookie.

"That is a beautiful dress you have on, girly." She cracked a crooked smile in my direction. "Did your mother sew it?"

My blood boiled at the mention of the woman who was nothing more than a name on a piece of paper in my life. She never gave me anything but my button nose and dark brown eyes I silently despised. They reminded my father too much of what once was, and that was just the beginning of his resentment toward me.

"No, I purchased it from the dress shop across from Celia's café." I smiled at the woman. My mother's shortcomings were not her fault, and I refused to take it out on her. Smoothing the light blue flower-petal design down on the dress, I watched as she admired it once more.

"Well, it is still just as beautiful. You tell your father that I loved his service today." She winked at me and hobbled off to another table which held some type of lemon tarts from Celia.

A piece of stray hair batted in the wind and into my eyes. I blew it away, but it soon floated back into my sight line.

"Still getting roped into these church functions, dear Claire?" A male's voice called out to me from a few feet in front of the table.

Peering up at the voice, I met the green eyes of Asher Faye. When I had first arrived in Idelwood, the Faye twins and Rowen Caldwell had been my first friends. Asher and Aspyn kept to themselves with the strange red headed boy, Finley Blackbourne, trailing behind them wherever they went. Most of the time I felt like the fourth wheel to their trio when I was around them. It always seemed like they had a huge secret that I wasn't allowed to be let in on. But Rowen had latched on to me and never let go. Not that I minded at all; she was kind and like a sister I never had.

"Well, if it isn't Asher, the troublemaker of town himself," I hollered back at him, placing both hands on my hips. He laughed at the comment but didn't deny it either. Everyone in town knew wherever his sister and he went, trouble found them. It was only one of the perks of being their friend. The other was it drove my father insane.

Asher raised an eyebrow at me. "Why did I believe you thought better of me?"

"Only repeating what everyone knows to be true." I smirked. "What are you doing here?"

"Oh, right." His cheerful mood dropped from his tone quickly. "Uh, Rowen wanted you to meet her at this address later."

He thrust out a torn piece of paper in my direction. I took it between my fingers and peered down at the address that was scrawled out in Rowen's handwriting.

"What's with the theatrics?" I laughed and shoved the note into the tip jar that currently sat empty on the table. "Why couldn't she just come meet me today?"

"It is a long story that I don't have the time or patience to get into," Asher grumbled. He shoved his hands into his jean pockets. "So, will you come?"

I nodded once to the boy. "Yeah, when does she want to see me?"

"Wednesday, right after the final school bell rings," Asher said. I confirmed once more I would be there before he walked away from me.

The bake sale wrapped up as soon as the sun began to melt into night. I sat at my father's desk in his office counting the money earned from the sale when a knock on the door caused me to lose my place.

"Come in," I called out, frustrated at whoever was behind the wooden door. A boy around my age stepped through the entryway. His skin was a natural tan color that you couldn't achieve in the sun even if you tried. Dark locks were curled underneath each other in a loose wave which he had styled into a perfect undone look. My breath caught in the back of my throat as he pushed through the doorway, not bothering to look up to meet my gaze.

"Can I help you?" I asked. My voice shook slightly as he silently stood in the room. His eyes snapped up to meet mine; they were a pale blue that matched the sky on a clear summer's day. Even in the dim office lighting, they stood out against the rest of his features.

He shot me a narrow look. "Where is your father?"

"Uh." I turned to look nervously at the clock hung to the right of us. "He didn't say when he would be back."

I stood from my spot, rounding the corner of the desk with my hand outstretched to introduce myself. "I am Claire Halloway by the way. I don't think we have officially met. You are?"

The boy scoffed at my hand, folding one arm over the other against his chest. "I know who you are. Everyone in town knows you, princess. You have to know that."

"There's no need to be rude." I glared at him. "You didn't tell me your name. I can let my father know you stopped by when he comes back."

"Just inform him that Gabriel Moreno stopped by. He'll get the message from that."

I stood there shocked at his blunt words. Gabriel turned and headed toward the door without another word. I followed him quickly, but his long strides made it difficult to keep up.

"Hey!" I shouted after him. "What is your issue?"

He ignored me, continuing down the aisle in the middle of the pews. I halted and watched him slip through the front entrance of the church without another word. Anger burned in the pit of my stomach at his behavior. I had never met someone who infuriated me with only a few words more than that boy had.

CHAPTER TWO

Bright light shone through the café's front windows. I had chosen my regular booth to sit in to complete the piles of schoolwork I had. Every Tuesday and Thursday since the day I had moved into Idelwood, I'd wandered over to Celia's to tackle homework I had acquired that day. It was easier than doing it on the slick wood of the pews while my father rehearsed his upcoming sermon for the hundredth time that day. Although the order of hot chocolate and a slice of apple pie wasn't a bad bribe either.

Today the café was almost completely empty other than a few older woman and a couple of lovesick teenagers who were sucking face in a booth. I scrunched my nose up in disgust as the guy shoved his tongue further into the girl's mouth. Both fighting for dominance over the kiss, but they just managed to look like two wet fish grappling for air on the surface.

"That is disgusting," Celia mumbled as she set down the slice of apple pie for me. "Here you go dear, your usual."

"Thank you, Celia." I smiled politely at the woman.

"You just let me know if you need anything else," she said, patting my shoulder once before walking back to the kitchen. My eyes followed her until she rounded the corner of the counter and disappeared into the back.

The science homework in front of me was getting on my last nerve as the textbook continued on about the anatomy of a frog. There would be a lab on dissecting the creature in a few days that I was desperately trying to get out of. My eyelids drooped slightly as I highlighted the text with a bright yellow marker.

"That looks riveting," a deep voice said. I

looked up to meet the gaze of Xander Caldwell. It was odd to see Xander in the café when so many people were around. Even though there were only a few patrons milling about, those few were usually too many for Xander to feel comfortable with. From the little I understood about Xander, people didn't like him in this town. Maybe it was the bad boy get-up he always had on or the fact that even him just sitting across from me made my blood turn to ice.

"Xander," I breathed out, "what are you doing here?"

"Rowen asked me to come find you." Xander leaned back against the plastic booth. I raised an eyebrow in response to his comment and waited for him continue. "She has been trying to find the time to come speak with you, but the internship she has with the town council takes up most of her time."

"I can imagine," I grumbled, looking back down at the science textbook. He didn't take the hint that I was not interested in continuing the conversation with him. Xander stayed planted in the booth across from me. Looking up to meet his eyes, I said, "What did Rowen need?'

It felt strange talking about her as if we were in an unannounced fight. Why Rowen couldn't find the time to pick up the phone to call or send a carrier pigeon to my father's office was beyond me. But it had been this way since she graduated last year along with most of my friends, leaving me alone in the hell that was high school.

"She wants to meet with you tomorrow." Xander watched me like he was examining me for a secret flaw that he planned to destroy.

I shrugged in response. "I got the message from Asher at the bake sale Sunday."

He flicked a ripped piece of notebook paper across the table, and it landed in the middle of the text I was currently highlighting. "The plans have changed since then. Here's the new address. See you at six tomorrow night."

With that he was out of the booth and moving with the shadows out of the café's door. I sighed, running one hand through my mess of hair that hung against my forehead. The café door slammed open once more, its glass paneling rattling as it hit the wall behind it. Aspyn Faye flew into the room, eyes wild with rage as she made her way around the counter and into the back room. I assumed she was going to hunt down Celia as it seemed those two were thick as thieves. It was most likely that the twins were going at it again like most of their days. It was a wonder neither of them had killed each other in their petty arguments.

I reached down and held the notebook paper Xander had tossed in front of me to read. The hair on the back of my neck stood up as I felt someone watching me. Slowly I set the paper back down and turned to meet the eyes of Gabriel who sat staring at me from across the booth behind me.

"Are you stalking me now?" I hissed toward him.

Gabriel smirked in response before he stood and began walking around to the other side of his booth. I turned around, not wanting to entertain him at all.

"You would never know if I was stalking you my dear." Gabriel's hot breath tickled the inside of my ear. I sucked in a breath as goosebumps rippled across my skin.

"What do you want?" I asked, my voice coming out in a forced whisper. Keeping completely still, I only turned my eyes to the left in order to see Gabriel watching me.

"Do I make you nervous, Claire?" Gabriel's voice was barely a whisper. I could see his gaze scan my figure, making my stomach flip. For some reason he made me nervous in the same dangerous way a predator stalks their prey before sucking the life out of them.

"No," I choked out. "You didn't answer my question."

Gabe's hand reached around me, his arm brushing up against mine as he grabbed the notebook paper.

"Hey." I turned into him to try to get the paper. My nose brushed up against his in the act and I realized how close we were. I stilled, eyes flicking to his lips and then back up to his pale blue gaze. "Give it back to me."

A beat passed, and neither of us moved. I knew

the patrons in the café were staring, but I couldn't find it in myself to care what they thought. If they decided to run back to tattle on me to my father, so be it. I was holding my breath, and the lack of air in my lungs left them burning with anticipation for my next move.

"Please," I begged. Gabriel moved back, much to my disappointment, and handed the paper to me. I took it between my shaky fingertips, the object feeling foreign in my hand.

"You shouldn't go," Gabriel stated. I thought I could hear concern lace his words. Meeting his eyes, I opened my mouth to ask why, but he spoke once again, "You should stay away from everyone connected with Xander Caldwell. He has a habit of ruining people just by association."

Gabriel stood from his place in his booth and began to walk away. I waited a few steps before calling out to him, "What about you? Should I stay away from you, Gabriel?"

He stopped but did not turn to meet my gaze. The muscles in the back of his neck tensed, the half of his face I could see was covered in shadows, but

I could still make out the grim line that his mouth was set in.

"Especially me, Claire." His words were harsh, leaving me feeling empty. I couldn't quite put my finger on why they made me feel this way. But I knew I had to find out.

The church was lit up when I made my way into it. Today was Tuesday, which meant more people than most nights were milling about the service hall to get things ready for the children's activities that occurred every Wednesday.

Mallory Manson stood at the front of the church, her blonde hair swinging from side to side as she spoke with another girl from our school year. The only way I could tell her, and Tabitha apart was the fact that Mallory always had a smile plastered across her face when she spoke to anyone. It was as if that person was her favorite one in the room in any given conversation. Her ice-blue eyes connected with mine, and she excused herself from the girl. I was in no mood to speak with anyone after my encounter with Gabriel, but there was nowhere to run and hide without being rude.

"Claire," Mallory said, her eyes bright with joy as she made her way in front of me. "Just the person I was looking for."

"Well, here I am," I said lamely, throwing my hands up in a fake surprised motion.

She chuckled at it. "I have something for you."

Her hands dug in a black purse she had slung over her shoulder. It only took her a moment to find what she was looking for. She thrust in my direction a small wooden box with large angel wings carved into the wood. I squinted at her suspiciously as she waited for me to take the object.

"I missed your birthday," Mallory explained as she held it out in front of her.

"My birthday is in June." I raised one eyebrow at her. She only shrugged and pushed the box toward me more forcefully this time.

"Just take the box, Claire." Mallory's voice dipped into a threatening whisper. The tone sent chills down my spine. I met her narrowed eyes before taking the wooden box in my shaking hands. The weight of the box was strangely lighter than what I expected it to be. Mallory's bubbly personality reappeared once more. "Well open it, silly."

I undid the clasp holding the lid closed. It let out what sounded like a hiss that caused me to jump at the sound. I looked back at Mallory, but she either didn't hear it or chose to ignore the noise altogether. Lying in the center of the box was a gold necklace with a single medallion on the chain. The gold shone even in the dimly lit room of the church. I picked it up between the pads of my fingers, holding it eye level with me. The metal felt as if it was pulsing underneath my touch, sending a light drum of power surging through my arm as it swung calmly in time.

"Mallory," I whispered, finally meeting her soft eyes. "It's beautiful. I can't accept this. It must have cost a fortune."

I tried to hand the necklace back to Mallory, but she stepped back from the jewelry piece with fear in her eyes. Searching the necklace for any reason it would cause her reaction, I couldn't see anything that indicated it wasn't a normal piece.

Or as normal as a necklace that pulsed under my touch could be.

"Put it on." Mallory's voice shook slightly. I watched her closely but did as she said. The clasp of the necklace latched together, allowing the medallion at the middle of the chain to hang just below my collarbone. "Don't take it off, Claire. Ever. It might just save your life."

"What do you mean?" I stroked the edge of the gold, letting the power surge in my veins once again. Mallory craned her neck behind her, meeting the eyes of an older man who was watching us very closely. She rushed away from me, leaving me with unanswered questions. I rolled my eyes and reached up to remove the necklace, but the clasp I had just closed was gone from the chain.

Spinning the necklace around in my fingers confirmed that the clasp was not attached to the piece, leaving the necklace trapped around my throat. I looked up to meet the eyes of the man who ran Mallory off. His face was red with anger as he noticed the jewelry piece attached to me. Letting my shaky hands come down to my sides, I broke eye contact with him before making my way into the back corner where my father's office sat.

The door was wide open like it was most nights we had volunteers in the church. It made my father look accessible to the congregation even though I knew he did not want to be disturbed. I knocked my fist against the wooden door to get his attention as I entered. The sour look he wore most days popped up to greet me. He sat behind a large wooden desk which spanned from one end of the room to the next.

"I just came by to see if you required my assistance on anything before I head home." I spoke as kindly as I could to the man I had no desire to be around.

His long talon-like finger beckoned me in. I stepped further in the office, bringing the door to a close as I did. It clicked shut, and we sat in silence for a long moment. My father watched me with judgment as the seconds ticked by.

"What is this I hear about you and Gabriel Moreno being together in that café in town square?"

The air around me began to heat with anger.

Someone had snitched to my father, just as I suspected they would. Nothing in Idelwood could stay a secret. Though that was a problem with most of the small towns I had lived in, this one in particular was the worst of them all.

"We were just talking." I wrung my fingers together behind my back.

He peered at me. "Hm, well I don't approve of that boy. I want you to stay away from him."

"I don't see how that is at all fair." I searched for any way to change his mind. "Gabriel has been nothing but kind to all of us. What do you expect me to do? Ignore him in public when he chooses to speak to me?"

My father's hand slammed against the desk, sending a sickening crack around the room. "I expect you to act like a girl who honors her commitment to this church. Not throw herself at any boy that comes her way like some cheap whore you buy off the corner."

I flinched at his words. He had high expectations I had no desire to meet, but until I escaped his roof, I had to act as if I did.

"No daughter of mine will be running around town with a boy who could be the brother to the devil himself." He grumbled to himself before settling back down into the work he had spread across the table. I took my chance to leave, slipping out the door as a single tear began to roll down my cheek.

Wiping furiously at the tear, I scrambled out of the church walls and into the forest surrounding the building. As I made my way over to the bridge, I felt eyes watching me from the tree line. Peering into the darkness, I made out a silhouette of a man. The figure did not unnerve me like I believed it should because I knew the eyes that watched me. Their pale blue scanned over me. I stepped forward but he retreated into the shadows with one nod in my direction before disappearing from my view.

Chapter Three

Gabriel's warning rang loudly in my ears as I approached a rundown trailer in the middle of the woods. The address on the notebook paper had led me directly to the edge of a gravel path. There was no other building around for miles other than the modular home. An uneasy feeling pulsed through my veins as I reached the door, and I couldn't help but think that maybe the boy who set the air on fire when he was near me was correct about not showing up.

Before my fist could reach the metal door, it swung open, revealing a smiling Rowen. She gathered me into a hug, just as she always had before she became distant.

"Claire." Her voice was muffled under the crook of my shoulder. Rowen pulled back. A glow surrounded her from the darkness that stood just behind her. "I am so glad you came."

"Of course. Why wouldn't I come?" I shifted my weight between my feet. Xander stepped out of the shadows, placing a hand on Rowen's shoulder. His face was set in a permanent scowl, and the tension that rolled off him wrapped its spiny fingers around my windpipe. I felt like I had been punched in the gut, breath coming uneven as the three of us stood together. "What is going on?"

Xander stepped around Rowen onto the small metal porch that was attached to the trailer. I stepped back, letting the short railing dig into my vertebrae. One wrong move and I could accidentally fling myself over the rail. The fall wouldn't kill me, but the look in Xander's cold eyes might.

"Claire," Rowen's soft voice called to me. "I have something to tell you, and I don't want you to freak out."

My eyes flicked between the pair. "Why does

this feel like this is something that is going to change everything?"

"Because it is," Xander said, scoffing as he looked at me. Rowen stepped closer to him, letting her hand trail down his muscled arm. The movement seemed to relax him, but I could still feel the hostility coating the evening air.

I pulled my lower lip between my teeth, gnawing on the surface before speaking up once again. "Well, go on then."

Rowen took a deep breath, closing her eyes as she began to speak. "This town is different, but I think anyone would realize that by just stepping into it. That's irrelevant in the grand scheme of things really, and what I am about to tell you can't be spread about. It is more for your safety than either of ours."

"You're rambling, love." Xander smirked down at the petite girl.

"I know, but it isn't every day we tell an outsider this." Rowen rolled her eyes at him. "Claire, you are living among Heaven's creatures and some of the damned as well."

Scrunching my eyebrows together, I waited for her to break into her musical laugh and say she was joking. That everything she was explaining was just her version of a prank, but it never came. Xander only stared, waiting for me to react to the lunacy that she had spewed at me.

"So, what you are telling me is that you two are celestial beings? Angels? The great ones who watch over the sinners?" I sneered at them, "Yeah right, and I am a mermaid when I jump into the river by the church."

Pushing myself away from the railing, I started to make my way down the rickety staircase. My body was jerked back by the force of a hand. I glared at Xander, who had a tight grip on my upper arm.

"What? Have you decided to tell me that you turn into a little red man with pointy horns at night?" I growled, pulling at the grip he had on me. It grew tighter as I mocked him, and the eyes that were always so vibrantly blue flashed to black. They were soulless, hypnotizing me with their threatening waves of shadows that were known to follow Xander.

"This is not a joke, Claire," Xander spit out through gritted teeth. I could feel my body begin to shake with terror as he drew me closer. "And I may be a demon in my own right, but the devil's once best friend seems to be cozying up to you without you even realizing it."

"Let me go," I pleaded, hoping that the fear in my voice was enough for this monster to release me. His eyes moved down to the medallion which was trapped between by breasts. Xander's other hand reached out, picking up the piece between his fingers, He twirled it around for a moment before dropping it back into place.

"Are you going to listen to what Rowen has to say?" Xander's eyes narrowed in on me. I simply nodded, not trusting my voice to not betray my lie. He removed his hand from my arm and stepped back toward Rowen.

"We need your help Claire," Rowen's voice was no more than a whisper.

"Help?" I shook my head. "What could you

need me for?"

"Rowen is with child," Xander said, but I refused to meet his gaze. The acid in my stomach burned the back of my throat.

"That doesn't explain why you would need me."

"Xander isn't like me, per se," Rowen began. "You see, he lost his wings a while back and because of that, this child shouldn't even exist. If anyone were to know about her, well, let's just say none of us would live to remember it."

I sucked in a shaky breath. What Rowen was saying was all too much for my brain to handle, but she continued on for the moments she had my attention. "We need you to agree to leave with her once she is born. Take her somewhere that she could live a happy life without someone trying to kill her every day. Once she is old enough, we'll decide how much she should know about us. If anything at all."

"I'm not even eighteen," I said, wringing my hands together in front of me. "And how would I outrun angels who are trying to kill your child?"

"We are still working out the plan, but I promise you would never be found." Xander's voice was hard with emotion. I finally met his eyes. They were back to their normal blue color. Each piece of them shone with a different emotion as they flashed through his mind.

I stepped back once again. "This...I...no." The words sputtered out of me as I turned away from the couple. I stumbled down the stairs, and this time they let me go. The night air, which was normally cool at this time of year, was hot and sticky against my skin. My lungs were screaming at me as I tried to swallow enough air, but nothing worked.

I crashed into my car door, legs burning from running, and I fumbled to get the key to unlock it. Flinging myself into the driver's seat, I wrenched the door closed and snapped the locks down to ensure no unwanted guest wandered in to speak with me again. I slammed my head down on the steering wheel, letting out a wheezing scream that sounded more like a toy with a broken squeaker than an actual emotion I was expressing.

Peeling myself from the wheel, I placed the key in the ignition and looked toward the rearview mirror. Behind me I could see Xander standing at the edge of the woods that led out to the trailer watching me. He didn't come any closer as I pulled away and left without another thought.

The soft glow of lanterns surrounded the church when I came upon it. The congregation had been decorating for the upcoming gathering for the children's program they were hosting. I knew my father would still be hiding away in his office like he always was. Although we did not get along most of the time, I trusted that if I told him what was lurking in the shadows of Idelwood, he would be able to help. The heavy words I had scrawled out in my journal felt as though they were ready to pull me under a cloud.

Writing had always been the escape I needed, a way of sorting out the thoughts which jumbled my mind together in a murky wave until I couldn't think anymore. But now the chicken scratch in the leather journal felt more like a burden than a breath of fresh air. The pressure against my lungs made the lights of the church waver in and out. I took a step forward, ready to confess everything to my father; he would know how to handle this. But a dark figure at the edge of the tree line caught my attention.

I whipped my head toward the figure, a pair of blue eyes stared at me. They watched me with a soft understanding that made me feel as if I could trust them. The figure was small, looking to be only around five feet on their good days. Behind them another figure emerged from the shadows, towering over the small frame. I took the feeling building in my chest as a sign to leave while I still could, dashing into the warmth of the church's sermon hall.

The room was empty, the soft sounds of a hymn playing in the background just as it always did. I made my way toward my father's office, but he emerged from it before I could reach him.

"Claire," he said in surprise, one eyebrow raising in question. "I thought you would be home by now."

I let out a shaky breath, and the pressure of what I was going to unleash on him knocked into my lungs. "This town is filled with God's creatures."

The statement flew from my lips, each word fire in the back of my throat. My father blinked at me like I had three eyes and then shook his head the way he always did when he was frustrated with me.

"Stop this nonsense, Claire. What if someone in the congregation were to hear you spout off this nonsense?" His words were laced with annoyance. "It would make our family look insane. Whoever filled your head with these lies has obviously been tainted by sin."

Behind him, the soft light of the church sent rainbow speckles onto the back wall from the holy water we always kept filled to the brim. Running a sweaty hand over the checkered pink dress I had put on that morning, I looked up to meet his eyes once more.

"You don't understand. This is not the devil's work or any other biblical satire you are trying to throw at this, Father. It is not something you can sweep under the rug like everything else in this town. I have seen them in the square," I hissed at him in a voice I didn't recognize. It held a conviction that I could see even surprised my own blood in front of me.

"You will not speak a word about this to anyone in this town, Claire. This is a childish delusion that will fade in time, but until then I can't have you scaring the locals with silly bedtime stories. That's all they are. All they will ever be." My father's tone matched my venom. I shook with anger against his calm nature, the kind that told me I was being lied to. He already knew what lurked in the shadows of this town, and he refused to admit it to his only daughter. Turning on his heel, he began to retreat back to his cave of an office, just as he always did when we argued. Whenever he knew I was right in the argument.

"We all know that in this town things don't stay buried, Father. You of all people should know that." I eyed him as he stopped in his tracks, keeping his back toward me as I continued to speak. "This will come out, and when it does, whose side will you stand with? The demons that lurk in the shadows or the angels trying to 'protect' the town? This will destroy our home if it stays hidden. Something has to be done, and if you won't do it, I will."

In one fluid movement, he turned around and charged toward me. The crack of a hand meeting skin sounded off in the silent church. I reached up to my left cheek, tears brimming the edge of my eyes as my father turned back and escaped into his office.

That night my dreams were filled with blue eyes and large wings connected to a male's face I couldn't quite recognize. His touch kept me grounded in the dreams until the sun rose and I shot from my bed. Emptiness seeped into my bones as I stared up at the barely lit ceiling of my room. The town I had once thought was just strange for the sake of bringing in tourists now was filled with monsters that were infiltrating my dreams. And for some reason, I didn't feel the urge to run from the monsters. No, I wanted to run toward it, even if my death was the only thing it could give me.

Chapter Four

To say I was exhausted was an understatement. When the nightmares weren't plaguing my dreams, my mind was running on a constant loop of what Rowen had revealed to me. The revelation had me looking at people I had known since I arrived in Idelwood with a microscopic lens. Just waiting for them to peel away the layer to divulge that they were a part of this town's secret. But no one had revealed themselves to be on either side of the line in the sand these creatures had drawn.

No one but the obvious group who hung close to Rowen and Xander's side. Those in the inner circle were avoiding me like the plague. I had tried to speak with Asher earlier in chemistry, but he had brushed me off with a cold warning look.

A cart full of books I pushed in between the library shelves let out a horrendous squeak in the silence. A few students at one of the large wooden tables looked over at the sound, sending murderous glares in my direction for interrupting their study session. I rolled my eyes before continuing to the history section, which sat in the back corner of the building.

Coming to a stop in front of the half empty shelf, I mindlessly began to place books on it. Choosing to be the librarian's assistant for the last class of the day was a no brainer when I was asked. It gave me a chance to escape into a world where girls in beautiful dresses were saved by the handsome prince. Just for this single hour I didn't have to be Claire Halloway, the perfect daughter to the town's preacher. My mind wandered back to the last few pages of the novel I had been reading before the supervising teacher asked me to shelve the final books on the cart while she ran to a staff meeting.

I reached up, placing the last of the books on the top shelf. One caught the lip of the wood, causing the pile to tumble back on top of me. I threw my arms over my head to shield myself, but my body was thrust to the side, allowing the books to tumble to ground in hard smacks.

"Thanks," I whispered, pulling myself away from the stranger's grip.

"Maybe they should get you a stool for the higher shelves," Gabriel's voice called out. He was propped up against the opposite bookcase, a lazy smile spread across his lips as he watched me.

"I am perfectly capable of reaching the top shelf without the assistance of some stool." I huffed toward him, bending down to pick up the fallen books. His looming presence hung over me, watching as I slowly examined each novel to put them back into order. I stood up, returning the books to their place before craning my neck in his direction. "Was there something you needed, Gabriel?"

"Don't play dense with me, Claire." He stepped forward in long drawn-out strides. I pressed myself against the cool wood behind me. Gabriel placed both hands against the shelves by my head, trapping in me in his grasp. "And my friends call me Gabe."

"We aren't friends," I hissed, tipping my chin at him in defiance.

His hand slid down to grip the underside of my chin lightly. "Considering Xander exposed our secret to an outsider, I think that constitutes as friendship."

Gabriel gave my chin a light squeeze before his hand found its place in his back pocket. I pushed away from the bookshelf and made my way toward the empty library cart once more. "I have no idea what you are insinuating. Now if you would excuse me, I have to get back to what I was doing."

His eyes trailed down to the empty cart. I gripped it tighter, making the tops of my knuckles turn stark white. He stepped out of my way, and I took my escape. I pushed the cart forward; the wheels caught on a rift in the awful gray, stained carpet. The cart lurched forward under my weight, sending me tumbling against it. My eyes widened as my temple plummeted toward the rusted metal of the old cart.

The collar of my dress was jerked back as Gabriel caught me inches from the corner and slammed me into his chest. His arm snaked around my midsection to steady me. I took a few shaky breaths, letting my spine press further into him.

"Is this going to be a common occurrence? Me saving you from normally harmless things?" Gabriel's breath was hot against my ear. A shiver traveled through my body, and there was no denying he felt it.

"As opposed to the dangerous creatures in this town?" I asked, voice coming out in shaky mess. He let out a low growl, the arm holding me tightened. I went to speak again, but a group of three girls walked past the book aisle. Holly, a girl with deep brown curly hair who was in my previous hour, sneered toward us.

"This is a library, you know." She looked at our position. "If you are going to make out, at least take it to the janitor's closet like the rest of us have the decency to do."

The other two girls giggled at her before they

sauntered off. Each one of them whispering back and forth, no doubt about who they were going to tell first about what they witnessed.

I let out a groan and threw my head back against Gabriel's chest. He chuckled. "I'm going to let you go. Can you handle not tripping over your own two feet for half a second?"

"Can you handle not being an ass?" I growled. He let his hand linger in place for a moment longer, dragging it across my stomach and against my hip. Another wave of chills rippled across my skin and hurried away from his touch. My hand gripped the cart which almost sent me to the hospital, and I started to push it toward the library's teachers' lounge. Gabriel followed me silently. I felt his burning gaze watching every move I made.

The door of the lounge swung open as I pushed the cart back into its place on the far wall. It was filled wall-to-wall with large industrial cabinets, with a printer and scanner in the center of the room. I moved around the electronics and opened the cabinet I stored my bookbag in.

"You can leave now," I called over my shoulder.

Reaching in my bag, I dug out the book I had been engrossed in before. Maybe if he left now, I could get in a few more pages in before the bell rang.

"Go see Celia at her café," Gabriel's voice called out. I dropped my book back into the bag, turning to see him standing in the doorway. "Tell her I sent you. She'll help you understand that not all of us are monsters."

My eyebrows pinched together in confusion. Before I could ask him what he meant by that, the bell sounded around us. Reaching back into the cabinet, I yanked my book bag out of the space, sending the contents of it flying across the floor.

"Geez, what is wrong with me today?" I groaned, bending down to gather my books off the floor. Gabriel was in front of me instantly, hands out to gather the fallen items up for me. Reaching out a hand, he placed a book on top of my pile. My eyes met his blue ones, lights in the room making them look paler than normal.

"Not all of us are monsters, Claire. Just a select few, and if they catch wind that you know our secret…" Gabriel's voice faltered. "Well, I don't want to find out what would happen to you. Let's just say that."

Then he stood up and was gone from the room before I could even respond.

Celia's café felt haunted by demons from the past today. Maybe it was because Idelwood's skies were covered in the darkest clouds I had ever witnessed. The sky lit up as the first strike of lightning erupted through the heavens, followed by the angry sound of thunder, making my heart race against my chest in painful spurts. I stepped into the café. The heel of my sneaker squeaked against the linoleum. Celia's bright eyes met mine, her movements halting mid-sweep as she took in my frazzled state.

"I was told to speak with you if I wanted to know the truth," I sputtered out, the words rushing from my lips in without pause. The woman's eyes widened, and I continued before she could tell me to get lost. "Gabri—Gabe sent me."

"I know," Celia smirked, leaning into the broom. My eyes wandered around the room, now painfully aware that someone could easily be sitting in one of the booths. She followed my stare. "Oh, don't worry, there's no one here. I closed early. We have been expecting you."

"We?" I questioned.

"Gabe told me he was going to send a certain preacher's daughter my way, and the ancestors are a bunch of gossips." Celia nudged her head to the left, indicating for me to sit at one of the barstools. "That boy is very protective of you."

I scoffed, "More like I am the bane of his existence."

Celia chuckled, taking a seat to my right, and letting the broom lean up against the counter between us. "What would you like to know, Claire? About the angels? The Fallen? Or how about the piece of jewelry you have hanging from your neck?"

"Everything. I wanted to know everything I could possibly need to understand about these creatures that I live with." I met her eyes with a determined stare.

"That could take a while. I will give you a

summarized version, though." Celia smirked at me, eyes watching my body language with laser focus.

"Angels, such as Abel and the council, have been on earth since before the text they are depicted in existed. From what I was taught by my mother, they founded Idelwood as a safe haven to conduct their business when the mortal's view on them soured. It was safer to dwell in a place they could control, especially with the mortals they allowed in."

She paused eyeing me for a reaction that would tell her to stop before continuing, "The twins and Gabe were a few select angels to arrive with the scarce title of being an Elite. I don't understand the process of how they are promoted to this role, but I know in the heavens it was a highly coveted title for many years. Abel has become lax in the past century on whom he allows to become an Elite. I believe he just wants to grow his ranks to a sizeable amount in the event war breaks out."

"Can they go back if they want?" I questioned, eyebrows raising with awe at what Celia was telling me. "To the heavens?"

"I have never seen it done, but that does not mean it is impossible." Celia removed a crumb from the countertop, "I just always assumed they enjoyed their role here earthside."

"And the mortals? Are we supposed to just accept the creatures who could obliterate us if we step a toe out of line? I don't see how that is at all fair. I can imagine not all mortals go easily when they are being controlled by these creatures, which means innocent bloodshed."

"You speak of them like they are only monsters in a child's bedtime story."

"Well, aren't they?" I asked, nose scrunching together as if I smelt something rotten as I thought of the angels and demons that filtered through this very café.

"No," Celia said, voice full of conviction. "And that necklace around your neck is proof that they care for people like you, even if they suffer the consequences. Yes, some can be cruel but aren't humans just as ruthless? They were not created to be evil, Claire, but ego and power have ruined some of them."

I reached up, my hand skimming the underside of the medallion. "Even though I grew up in the church, I feel as though I know nothing about what I am being thrown into. Have you ever heard my father preach the Garden of Eden story? I am pretty sure he embellishes it even more each time he gives a sermon on it."

"Can't say I have." Celia smiled, the sides of her eyes crinkling. "Might have to request it for a Sunday service just so I can witness it."

"Please don't put us through that again." I giggled. "I do have one question that I haven't been able to wrap my mind around."

"Ask away."

I gulped in a deep breath, "Besides Abel and the council, how old is everyone in Idelwood?"

"Old," Celia chuckled. "Most of the angels in this town were around during the creation—Gabriel included—but they are set in a prime age here on earth to blend with the mortals. I am much older than I appear as well. My family has been the Keepers of heaven's creatures since the year was described as BC in your history book, and we only grasped the surface of what we were protecting. I was born in 1542."

"That would mean you are...." I gawked, braining trying to add up the number mentally.

"Old. Like I said." Celia winked at me. "But I stay looking at the age of 26, the same age I took my title, which is much better than over 400."

I stared at her, taking in her smooth skin to find a flaw that would indicate her true age. "But how is that possible?"

"Keepers are always female; it is believed we have a more level-headed outlook about the artifacts we protect and how their owners should use them, but the men in our lives are considered our scholars, equally as important but without the added power benefits." Celia's face had grown solemn, a deep crease appearing between her brows as she began to recant the past to me. "Turmoil had been brewing between the heavens and the Keepers the month of the massacre. My mother hadn't stopped pacing the square of her study for days, and I knew the tension was about to come to a boiling point soon. But I didn't know it was going to be that night."

A single finger began to tap on the counter, her eyes glazing over in a trance. "My father had sent me out to fetch a buddle of wood. It was an abnormally cold night for the time of year. I felt the power rush into me before I saw the blood-stained walls. My mother's head was on a spike in the middle of our kitchen, and for the first time in my life, I was alone. There are other Keepers from smaller circles, but ours was considered royalty to the Elite. I became the one of the youngest Keepers to obtain that magnitude of power that night, frozen in time until I grant my powers to another, or it is ripped from me through death."

I sucked in a shaky breath. "And the Elite, they are older than you?"

"In a sense," Celia said, nodding. "They are frozen like I am in a prime age here on earth. This age was chosen well before they had the chance to think about it when they were given the honor of becoming an Elite Angel. The Faye twins, for example, look to be around eighteen, but their souls are older than time can even comprehend. This is true for all the Elite in Idelwood."

"Wow," I whispered, trying to rack my head around being in existence for as long as the creatures of this town had been. "You said that they cared because of my necklace? Mallory Manson claimed I was never be able to take it off until the time was right. Not that I haven't tried to remove this piece of junk from my neck. It has fused itself around my neck like my own personal noose."

"That piece of junk was forged from the Ark of the Covenant and is one of the oldest artifacts in The Crypts," Celia explained. I opened my mouth, ready to apologize for my insult, but she held up a hand, silencing my words. "It will protect you from any meddling ethereal beings. They would be stuck down and burned by hellfire if they tried to harm you with that hanging around your neck."

I gulped in my nerves. "And will they still try?"

"Mercilessly."

Chapter Five

The brisk morning air tickled my bare legs as I made my way through the oldest part of Idelwood's cemetery. A large mausoleum towered over the broken tombstones that were scattered around the dead grass. The structure blocked the rising sun, leaving a misty glow to float around the graveyard. After another nightmare filled with wings and a baby's cry that still rang in my ears, I had called Rowen.

Leaned up against one of the pillars of the mausoleum was Xander. I'd expected him to show up alone, but as I drew closer, the blonde hair of Mallory Manson floated around in the wind on the other side of Xander. Stopping at the steps of the structure, I looked up at the pair. Mallory turned to me first. Her once pale gray eyes now held a vibrant glow that matched Xander's. Mallory's gaze connected with the medallion lying on my chest. She flinched slightly before turning away from me entirely.

"Rowen was glad you finally called." Xander kept his back to me, watching a swaying tree just to the right of us.

I shifted uncomfortably back and forth at his comment. "And you?"

The muscles in his jaw tightened, and I could almost feel the tension in his body coiling up like a rattlesnake. Ready to strike against anyone who came too close. Xander turned his head toward me, taking in my stance at the end of the stairs. "That all depends on what you decide right now."

Mallory started around the man, and the usual jump in her step replaced the tense look she'd just had. "Xander you are scaring her. Give the poor girl a break. She just found out monsters are real and living in her normal town."

"Idelwood has never been classified as normal to me," I said, a small smile forming on my face. Mallory threw her arms around my neck, enveloping me in a warm hug.

"I suppose you are right about that, Claire." Mallory giggled. I gave into the hug, squeezing the girl against me. Mallory pulled back abruptly and hissed in pain. Her left hand reached over her shoulder to rub the muscles of her back. She gave me a weak smile. "Sorry, I am still a tad sore from my wings getting ripped out of my back."

Stepping back, I gaped at her in horror. She seemed so normal for having just been robbed of a vital piece of her existence.

Xander fully turned around, facing both of us. "We don't have time for this, Mallory."

"We never have time to live, Xander." Mallory glared at him.

The tension was thick in the air, but I knew I had to say what I had been thinking about all morning. After speaking with Celia my perspective of these creatures had been altered. I was about to give myself over to something that would never benefit me, but instead most likely get me killed.

"I will help you and Rowen," I said, staring

directly into the vibrant blue eyes of the fallen angel. "No questions asked. I know this could get me killed, but I think whatever is going to happen is bigger than any of us. So, I will do whatever you need me to do."

Xander's eyes narrowed, waiting for me to take back what I just said, but it never came. The sound around us was filled with the whistle of the wind weaving through the dead as we disturbed their peace.

"Are you sure?" Mallory asked, one hand reaching out to comfort me.

"No." I stepped away from her touch, clutching the skirt of my pale blue dress. I wrung the fabric together to keep my hands from shaking as I spoke. "But it is the right thing to do. And sometimes following the crueler path in life is easier than dying a coward."

A storm brewed in the distance as I followed the dirt path home. The sky, which was normally a bright blue color at this time of day, was a smoky gray. A strong scent of rain hung in the air as I kicked a rock down the path. It bounced a few feet in front of me before I performed the action over again. The front gate of my house was swinging back and forth in the wind when I finally made it home. The faulty latch would send the gate flying open with just a simple touch most of the time.

The wind was becoming violent, kicking up dust and leaves that were scattered across the yard. My head was yanked to the side, and the white ribbon in my hair was thrust into the wind. I watched it float across the yard and into the forest before it caught on a rogue tree branch.

Huffing in annoyance, I trudged through the side yard to where the ribbon was caught. I was only a few steps away from the fabric when a bony hand reached out from the darkness of the trees and tore the white ribbon from its branch. Stopping in my tracks, I stared at where the hand had once been, but not even the bushes behind the tree showed any signs of another person around.

The ribbon floated back through the tree line and into the roaring wind. I reached out quickly, snatching the fabric out of the air. Then I noticed the once white ribbon was now a bright red color and sticky to the touch. The color was dripping off the end as it if it had been freshly dipped in a paint can, but the metallic smell that hung around the air made my stomach twist in disgust.

"That is my ribbon," a young girl's voice called out to me. I peeled my gaze away from the hair piece and looked to where the voice came from. A small child no more than eight stood staring at me from the edge of the trees. She was wearing a white nightgown that was stained down the middle with the same red color as the ribbon. Her hand was outstretched in front of her, waiting for me to give her back my ribbon. There was clear rotting happening on the left side of her body. It started at the tips of her fingers which had no skin left on them, and was beginning to travel up the rest of her body.

"Or we could play a game?" She cocked her head to the side, examining me carefully. "You could hide, and I could seek. If I find you, then I get my ribbon back, but if I give up, you can have it."

The girl took a step forward, coming just a few inches away from where I stood frozen. She eyed the ribbon with admiration. "Though I do hope I win, it is such a pretty thing."

I shoved the ribbon toward her. "You can just have it."

She didn't take the ribbon, just stared at me with narrowed eyes. "But I want to play a game with you, Claire."

The air in my lungs vanished as she spoke my name. I shook my head, stepping away from her, but her bony hand shot out and clamped down on my wrist with an iron grip.

"No!" I screamed and ripped my hand away from her with so much force it thew me onto my back. I scrambled away from her as she looked down at me like something she wanted to eat. The red on her dress seemed to darken into a deeper shade as it dripped off the fabric in large drops and onto my skin. I gasped. The liquid felt as if it was burning through my skin, creating large holes in my arms.

I clumsily got to my feet and raced away from

the girl. The sounds of her stomping behind me made me pick up my pace. I flew through the open gate and into the road. The headlights of a car swirled in front of me. I managed to step off the dirt road before the car sent my body crunching against its hood.

Large water droplets began to downpour from the sky, but they were hot and sticky. I reached up and wiped the liquid from my face with the back of my hand, only making it worse. My knuckles were red—the rain coming down wasn't rain at all. No, it was thick blood splattering against my face. I let out a horrified scream as I caught sight of the blood-covered girl making her way toward me in long drawn-out strides.

Staggering back, I began to run into the open lot behind me. The untamed brush tore through my legs, and I could feel the blood beginning to pool down them. Hands clamped down on my shoulders, pulling me to a stop. I thrashed against the grip, letting out a horrified scream as the figure turned me around to face them.

"CLAIRE!" the figure screamed at me, and

I stopped thrashing against them. Through the heavy rain I could make out a drenched Gabriel, concern lacing his features as he examined me. I craned my head around to peer over his shoulder to see if the girl was anywhere to be seen. Just outside the field she stood, blood pooling from her eyes as she gave me a haunting grin. The girl lifted one bony hand and waved before disappearing into thin air.

I let out a strangled sob and threw myself into Gabriel. His arms circled around my body, pulling me close to his warmth.

"You're freezing, Claire," he mumbled into my hair. "Let's get you cleaned up and into something dry before you get sick."

I just nodded. My eyes still trained on where the bloody girl had been taunting me.

Chapter Six

Gabriel's living room was empty. Actually, the entire home looked as if he had just moved into the place. In the front room there was a tan couch which faced a stone fireplace. I looked around the empty room as I waited for Gabriel to come back with the first-aid kit. The sounds of the crackling fire were interrupted by a crash of thunder, the noise feeling as though it rattled the entire house.

"I thought I was going to be done saving you from yourself for a while." Gabriel's voice startled me as he came around the dark corner of the hallway. I jumped, throwing my body into the cushions of the couch. He rushed forward, holding out a hand as if he were calming a crazed animal in the wild. I was sure I looked the part. His voice was soft when he spoke again. "Hey, you're safe now."

I nodded, gulping in a deep breath. "She just vanished into thin air. One moment she was behind me and then..."

Trailing off, I met Gabriel's concerned eyes. He held my stare for a moment longer before it traveled down to the cuts and dried blood on my legs. "Let me clean those up, and then we will figure out everything. I promise."

Promise.

The word felt foreign in the air when it came from his lips, but it made my entire body fill with a strange warmness. He didn't wait for me to respond before grasping underneath both of my legs and placing them on top of his thighs. I let out a hiss of pain as he dabbed the wounds with a wet washcloth.

"Sorry," Gabriel mumbled, quickly moving to dress the wounds with gauze and tape. Once he was done, Gabe sent me a quick smile. "There. All patched up."

"Thank you," I whispered, blood rushing to my cheeks as his fingers lightly trailed against my cheekbone. The touch felt electrified, like when two magnets fly together because they can't be apart any longer. My entire body shivered, not because of the damp dress that was stuck to my skin but instead because of the boy sitting in front of me.

"We should get you into something dry," Gabriel said, pulling his touch from my cheek and standing from his spot on the couch. He reached out the same hand, and I took it in mine without hesitation. Turning on his heel, he led me to the back of the house where a bedroom was dimly lit.

The room was drastically different from the rest of the home. It was furnished with a large wood bed and a matching dresser that sat opposite of it. A wool blanket was loosely tossed over dark sheets while the walls were covered in framed artwork. Most of them seemed to be hand drawn with a charcoal pencil. The room was warm and inviting, rather than the cold and dark feel of the rest of the home.

Gabriel removed his hand from mine and disappeared into a large closet on the opposite side of the room. He shuffled around for a moment before reappearing with a piece of clothing in his hands.

"Here," he said, handing a pair of sweatpants and a sweatshirt. "Change and then we can talk. Deal?"

I nodded. "Deal."

I had to roll the sweatpants waistband up a few times to keep them from falling down, and even then, they still dragged on the floor. Shuffling into the hallway, I followed the sound of running water into a small kitchen. A single barstool sat on the opposite end of an island. Gabriel stood with his back to me washing a coffee cup in the sink. I cleared my throat to make my presence known.

"I made tea," he called over his shoulder. "Thought it might warm you up more."

"You didn't have to do that." I stepped further into the kitchen.

He turned to look at me over his shoulder, a smirk plastered across his face. "I know, but I wouldn't want you to catch a cold. I heard those can kill humans, and you are prone to life-threatening situations."

"Oh yeah, laugh it up, Gabriel." I rolled my eyes, taking a seat on the stool. "Sorry my human tendencies bother such an immortal being as yourself."

He barked out a deep laugh. "They don't bother me. I find them refreshing actually. After a while, the immortal being business becomes boring."

"I'm sure," I said, letting out a laugh of my own at how utterly ridiculous this conversation was. Here I sat across from an angel. One that I had been warned to stay away from, but there was an electrifying feeling I couldn't help but cling to when I was around him.

The same coffee cup that he had just been washing slid in front of me. It was now steaming with what smelled like peppermint tea. I pulled the mug closer and let the warmth of the cup heat my cold hands. Gabriel leaned on the counter next to me, watching my every move with such intensity that it made me feel like an animal in the zoo.

"What happened out there, Claire?" Gabriel's voice was soft but firm. The violent rain against the kitchen window caught my attention. It reminded me of the thick blood that I had been caught in.

I held back a shaky breath as I turned back to him. "There was this girl, and she was covered in blood. It was raining blood, and she was chasing me. I—"

Hot tears rolled down my cheeks as I watched the incident play back in my mind. Gabriel's brows furrowed at my words. I could practically see the wheels turning in his head as he examined them.

"Claire," he began, "there was no one there. I heard you scream, but I didn't see anyone chasing you."

"I'm losing my mind." I stared past him, my eyes glazing over slightly as I remembered the stories my father told me of my mother and her episodes. "It runs in the family, you know. Seeing things that aren't actually there."

"I believe you," Gabriel spoke firmly. My eyes

darted back to his, waiting for him to give away that he was lying. He stared back, determination set in his gaze. "I believe you, Claire. If someone from the council assumed you may know something, they could be trying to scare you with these visions. Or simply trying to drive you out of your mind so no one would listen to you even if you decided to speak out."

I sighed, taking a sip of the hot liquid. It felt good to warm the chill that was set deep inside me. If the council knew, that meant I was going to need to be more careful with who I was around. Make it appear that I was just as oblivious as I once was.

"I have something of yours." Gabriel turned around, reaching into a drawer behind him. He pulled out a leather-bound journal, the one my father had bought for me this past birthday. I gasped as I snatched it from his hands. "You dropped it the other day in the library. I didn't think you wanted anyone to get their hands on it."

"Thank you, Gabe." I launched myself at him, throwing my arms around him in a tight hug. Gabe's arms snaked around my middle, pulling me close.

"No problem." He chuckled. I pulled back, looking at the crooked grin that was spread across his face.

"Now that you finally called me Gabe, you can write all about your infatuation with me and the raining blood."

I shoved myself away from him, anger bubbling in the pit in my stomach. Standing from my spot on the stool, it slammed to the ground from the force. I began to stalk away from him, but my steps were halted by his hand on my shoulder.

"Claire, I'm sor—" Gabe began.

"Don't," I interrupted him, bitterness seeping into my tone. "Don't apologize. I should have known. You told me to stay away from you, and I know why now because every time I start to think you are a good guy, Gabriel, you prove me wrong. And I don't want to get wrapped up with the bad guy."

His hand slid from my shoulder, and he let me sprint out of the house. The rain pelted down on me as I pulled the sweatshirt's hood over my head, sending the intoxicating scent of cedarwood and oranges into my nostrils. I turned back to look at the house once more, and only the darkness of the empty hall stared back at me.

Chapter Seven

I had watched at the same wood paneled door all week, expecting to catch Gabe watching back. But that never occurred. In fact, Gabe had vanished from my life completely. It was like he was a dream that I had conjured up when I was in danger to cope.

Saturday night I was finally done obsessing over a boy I never had a chance with. Our worlds were too different. Staring in the bathroom mirror, I smoothed down the dark jeans I had dug out of the back of my dresser. Jeans and I never really mixed, but tonight I was going for a look outside of my comfort zone. Something that didn't scream normal for Claire Halloway. If the jeans didn't show a new side of me, then the black tank top that was showing off more cleavage than I even knew I had would do the trick.

Throwing on a denim jacket, I headed downstairs to the door. My father sat in the front dining room, and I waited for a lecture on my outfit, but the only thing I got was a mumbled goodbye before he dove back into the notes he was taking.

There was a house party tonight, just as there was every weekend. If the teens of Idelwood were good at one thing, it was throwing parties. The last one I had been to was just before school had started in the middle of the forest on the outskirts of town. I had stood awkwardly off to the side watching my peers get obliterated while I swirled around a plain Coke. It was miserable. I had felt like the biggest loser in the world, too scared to let loose on the off-chance word got back to my father. But tonight, I was done with that fear.

My sneakers crunched against the gravel road, leading to the neighborhood connected just behind mine. I could already hear the pulsating bass of the music coming from the house. The entire structure was lit from top to bottom. Underaged kids spilled out onto the grass out front. As I walked past them, I could smell the joint they were passing around.

Pushing past the couple making out in the doorway, I stepped into a party that was much larger than those that were usually held. The house was dark with only the colorful lights from a rotating disco ball sitting in the middle of a random card table to illuminate the way. People were packed into the space like sardines, making it difficult to reach the kitchen at the back of the home. There was a thin layer of beer submerging broken bottles and cans on the floor.

Sidestepping a few of them, I picked up a random unopened beer from a cooler on the counter. The taste was disgusting, a mix between dirt and what I imagined a skunk's spray would taste like. I ignored the taste, throwing back the liquid as quickly as I could before tossing the bottle with its floating friends. Gripping onto a bright pink bottle this time, I made my way into a dark hallway which led to the other side of the living room.

It felt like hours as I stood leaned up against the back wall of the room, watching a few football players participate in the most intense game of beer pong I had ever seen. Lifting the pink drink to my lips over and over again, my vision was beginning to become hazy as the disco ball's colors melded together into a misty dream. I jumped as a strong hand gripped down on my shoulder.

I squinted up at them, trying to make my vision focus quicker. When it finally did, I found Asher Faye and Delaney Manson glaring at me.

"Hey guys," I said, my voice sounding an octave higher than usual. Asher's eyes narrowed at the empty bottle in my right hand. "What are you doing here?'

"I think a better question is what are *you* doing here, Claire?" Delaney leaned forward and snatched the bottle from my hand.

I furrowed my brow at her.

She looked back up at me. "Don't give me that look."

"I'm having fun. Did agreeing to help Xander and your little cult also include no fun?" I tried to step closer to them, but my feet moved quicker than my brain, causing me to stumble into Asher.

"Claire," Asher growled, catching my arms and steading me on my feet. "You are supposed to be keeping a low profile."

"I never agreed to that." I waved a finger in his face. Asher caught it in his hand—I pulled, but his grip kept it where he had it. "Hey, let me go!"

"We are taking you home." Delaney rolled her eyes at me. "Then you can explain why Aspyn is refusing to speak to any of us after that little meeting you two had today."

I narrowed my eyes at her. "I didn't meet with Aspyn today."

"Yes, you did." Asher looked at me curiously, finally dropping my hand. I shook my head at him. It wasn't possible for me to meet with Aspyn. I had been home all day sitting on the porch swing and failing at reading the required literature for school. My thoughts were too focused on Gabe's door. "Well, if you didn't meet with her, who did? Your ghost?"

"Maybe. I have heard and seen crazier in this

town," I screamed over the music as it reached the crescendo of the song. "Look, I'm not leaving. I told myself I was going to have fun tonight and that is what I am going to do."

I stepped around the two of them. Surprisingly neither of them followed me, and I wandered back into the kitchen. I was about to grab another bottle of alcohol when a hand tapped me on my shoulder.

"Asher, I told you—" I whipped around ready to tell the angel off, but instead a tall blond boy stood behind me. I knew him from my science class; his name was Leo, and for the most part he kept to himself unless around the football team. "Oh, sorry. I thought you were someone else."

"That's alright. Need me to talk to whoever is bothering you?" Leo winked down at me. My entire face flushed red at the action. He had never given me the time of day, but now standing in the dimly lit kitchen, I could see he was rather attractive.

"Uh, no. I think I can handle myself." I smiled up at him, moving a piece of hair behind my ear.

Leo motioned toward the backyard. "Here, let me get you a drink."

I only nodded and took his outstretched hand. We weaved between different people before making it out onto the wooden porch where a keg sat in the corner.

"Stay here," Leo said, removing his hand from mine and making his way over to the keg. Multiple members of the varsity team stood around the porch. They slapped him on the back as he neared. Almost in a congratulatory way. I shifted my gaze to the yard. In the darkness my vision created different shapes that swirled around in a synchronized dance.

"Here." Leo reappeared in front of me, a red solo cup held out for me to take. I pulled it close to my chest as he began to sip from his. "So, did you have to sneak out to come here?"

"Nope. Just walked out the front door," I said bitterly, already annoyed at his assumption. "My father doesn't control every move I make."

"Good." Leo stepped forward, his towering frame looming over mine. I inched back, my spine pressing into the brick of the house. Opening my mouth to say something about his closeness, I was cut off by someone calling him from inside the house. "Stay here, I'll be right back. It's probably one of the guys saying we need to make another beer run."

He dashed through the open sliding glass door and out of sight. My shoulders slumped, grateful for whatever drunk teen who had taken his attention from me. I lifted the drink to my lips, but it disappeared before they met the cup.

"Hey," I said, turning to the tall figure to my left. The red solo cup was crunched in Gabe's grasp, sending liquid spilling over the top and onto his hands. I rolled my eyes at him. "I don't need saving tonight, so you are off the hook."

"I beg to differ," Gabe grumbled, his eyes flaming with rage as he tossed the cup over the porch's edge.

"Well, I have no interest in speaking to you," I hissed. He stood unwavering as I shoved past him and into the still lively party. Weaving through the crowded room, I could feel Gabe following me. The same couple from hours earlier were still pressed up against each other, faces stuck together in a drunken mess. I grimaced racing out into the road as the boy let out a muffled groan.

We made it back to our street a few minutes later. My house was dark, and I could easily sneak in without getting caught if I was quiet enough. A better option would be to sleep on the old wooden porch swing until the sun came up and I was sober.

I whirled around to find Gabe standing just a few feet behind me. My thoughts were still muddled from the alcohol as I tried to come up with a way to escape from the conversation I knew was about to happen.

"You can leave now. I am sure I can manage to avoid danger from here." I turned my gaze back to the porch swing that would definitely leave my back in shambles in the morning.

"You are not going to sleep on that swing, Claire." Gabe said. I turned back to him as he shoved his hands in the front pockets of his jeans. Narrowing my eyes at him, I took a clumsy step forward. The toe of my sneaker caught a pothole, sending me tumbling toward the asphalt. Gabe caught me before I managed to faceplant.

I squirmed out of his touch. "I don't need someone like you saving me."

"Someone like me?" Gabe lifted one eyebrow in question. "What does that exactly mean?"

"It means that you're not a good guy." I stopped resisting his touch and looked up to meet his eyes. "One second you care, and then the next you're an asshole. I have a feeling you prefer to be the second one most of the time."

"I warned you to stay away from me and people like Xander, but you couldn't listen, now, could you?" Gabe glared down at me, his words coming out through clenched teeth. I ripped myself from his grasp, standing tall against his venom with my own.

"Do you think I had a choice?" I shouted. "Xander had me cornered between helping them and dying because of the knowledge he forced upon me. What do you suppose I should have done?"

Gabe just watched me. His eyes were filled with rage at my words. I huffed out a furious sigh. "That's what I thought."

I began to walk towards the front porch, my entire body becoming numb with each step away from him. I stole one more glance at Gabe. He still stood frozen with rage.

"And to think I was beginning to have feelings for you," I whispered. A single tear slid down my cheek as I gripped down on the metal gate and pushed forward. Before I could cross the yard, my body was spun around, and Gabe's lips were on mine.

His kiss was rough, filled with passion and emotion. I reached up, gripping the front of his black T-shirt, and pulled my body closer to his. His footsteps began to travel backward, and I followed willingly, our lips still connected. I don't know how we made it into his house, but I didn't really care as long as he kept his lips on me.

Gabe moved his mouth toward my jawline, nipping lightly at my neck and shoulder as he traveled down. I shivered under his touch as my head lolled back in pleasure. Removing my hand from his shirt, I pulled his face back up to mine. He growled into the kiss, making me smirk. We began to make our way into the back corner where his bedroom was with slow, lazy strides.

In that moment I knew one thing was for sure. If there was a poison that destroyed a girl such as me, then this boy was surely it.

Chapter Eight

My head felt like it had been hit by a brick the next morning as the sun shone into my eyes. I groaned, tossing over to avoid the rays, but my body collided with a solid form. I froze, eyes slowly opening to see my hand lying softly on the rising and falling naked chest of the boy I swore I would not give into. Gabe's eyes were closed, but his lips were quirked up in a devilish smirk.

"It's not polite to stare." Gabe's voice was rough. The tone sent a blush burning across my cheeks. I sank down into the bed, taking the blanket with me to cover my face in hopes it would conceal my embarrassment. A deep chuckle sounded above me.

"Shut up, you prick," I mumbled, the blanket

muffling most of the sound. Gabe shifted beside me, and before I could get a tighter grip on the blanket, it was thrown away from my face, and I was staring at him once again.

Gabe leaned down, his hot breath tickling my ear. "That's not what you had to say last night."

I gasped, pushing against his broad chest so I could glare at him better. "You take that back! All I did was kiss you."

Gabe's smirk deepened and he hummed a mocking reply. I felt my face pale at the sound. "Right?"

"I would tell you if there was more, love," Gabe said, a hand coming up and brushing away a curled piece of hair from my face. His touch lingered against my cheek for a moment. "Claire, I want to apologize for my actions the other day. I should not have made a joke about your journal. It was cruel."

My gaze faltered from his, thinking back on the words that had made my skin boil with rage. I opened my mouth to assure him it was okay, but immediately shut it because in reality it wasn't okay, and I didn't know how to tell him that without ruining everything.

"You don't have to say anything." Gabe's husky voice spoke softly, mouth sweeping up against my exposed shoulder. "But I hope it doesn't change what we decide this is."

Turning quickly, my nose brushed against his. The breath caught in the back of my throat making the words come out in a breathy whisper. "It doesn't change anything. Just don't let it happen again."

Gabe chuckled. "Never again, sweetheart."

Monday morning, everything was going wrong. My alarm didn't go off, and I burned my breakfast so badly it set off our smoke alarm. As soon as I stepped off my front porch, the rain poured down in heavy drops. I sighed, already wanting the school day to be over so I could curl up with my favorite book and a cup of tea in the back of the church.

A puddle splashed as I stepped in it, covering the bottom of my dress with murky rainwater. I groaned and glanced down at my watch to see if I had time to change. I didn't.

"You know we don't have to torture ourselves

with the mediocrity of our classmates' company today," a familiar deep voice called out in front of me. Leaning up against a blue pickup truck, Gabe stood watching me with a smirk.

"Some of us enjoy the company of non-angelic figures every now and again," I said, lips quirking up at the annoyance covering his face.

"I was going to offer you a ride to hell, but I think you deserve to walk like all the other heathens." Gabe turned around, swinging open the driver's side door. I rushed forward, ignoring the water that was now soaking my skirt. He threw me a look over his shoulder.

"What's one more devil in my life?"

The ride to school was filled with the soft patter of rain on the truck. It never felt uncomfortable with Gabe around. Being near him seemed to fill the missing void my heart longed for. I could have sat in the cab of his truck for hours without even questioning it. The brick building of the high school came into view. Even with the rain, the parking lot was swarming with students. I stared at a group on the other side of lot, making eye contact with Asher.

His eyes narrowed at me as Gabe opened my door.

"Ready?" he asked quietly. I tore my gaze from Asher. Gabe shook his head at the interaction. "Well, it seems that we have caused a rift in someone's morning."

I exited the truck, adjusting the strap of my bag on my shoulder. Gabe placed his hand on my lower back as we began to walk toward the school. It felt like every eye in the parking lot was burning into me as we moved, and I shrank closer to Gabe's warmth.

"I think I should have taken your suggestion of ditching this morning."

Gabe let out a loud laugh. "This is the closest thing to Lucifer himself rising from hell that any of these teens will get to."

"What is that supposed to mean?" I craned my neck up to look at him. He kept his eyes trained forward, continuing our journey to the entrance with steady steps.

"The council would have my wings just because I breathed the wrong way," Gabe said as he pushed open the double doors. Warm air followed by more shocked expressions greeted us, causing my cheeks to heat. "And this. Me parading around with someone who is forbidden to know what hides in this town...Let's just say they are going to implode on themselves when they catch wind of it."

We arrived in front of my locker before I spoke again. "They think you are as bad as the devil himself?"

My brows furrowed at the question. Gabe had his moments that made him look like a complete jerk, but nothing close to the devil that my father shouted about on Sunday mornings. Gabe leaned one shoulder against the locker next to mine, arms crossed in front of him and a deep frown resting on his lips.

"No." Gabe reached out, moving a damp piece of hair out of my face. "They find me worse, as having his oldest friend as one of their Elites can be problematic."

The warning bell rung, cutting through the shock that was racking my body. Gabe leaned down, brushing a kiss against my hairline. "You should get to class. I'll meet you for lunch."

Nodding numbly, I watched him walk away,

the sea of teens practically leaping out of his way to make a path for him. My stomach churned with anxiety. What had I tangled myself in? There was still so much that I was not aware of when it came to Gabe, but I was willing to push that aside for just another stolen moment between us.

The final bell rang as I slid into my seat in front of Asher. Our English teacher was out for the day, leaving us with a sub who instructed us to use this hour as a study period. It looked like he just didn't want to teach the lesson that was left for us and instead continued to read a tattered copy of *The Catcher in the Rye*.

The heat of Asher's glare pulsed on my neck. I sat rigidly waiting for him to speak, but he never did. Turning around, I eyed him. "Well, get on with it, will you?"

"What do you think you are doing?" Asher hissed at me. Delaney inched closer to us, watching every movement in case she had to intervene. Her face held the same annoyance as Asher's did when she caught me staring.

"I don't know what you are talking about," I

snapped. "Xander didn't give me a handbook of rules that I was expected to follow."

Asher leaned in, hands slapping the wood of the desk in front of him. Several students turned to look at us, but none stayed watching for long. His words came through clenched teeth. "No. But he did tell you to stay off the council's radar. Walking into school with him is not doing that. Now every council member will be sniffing around you to see what you know."

"Let them," I mumbled. Asher let out a low growl at my words. Delaney pushed a hand against his shoulder, trying to pull him from the conversation. Anger bubbled around us in thick heavy globs. Leaning closer to him, I glared at the two angels with all the courage I could gather.

"I would rather burn for the rest of my days than sit around waiting for heaven to catch me."

CHAPTER NINE

Rain continued for days, and by Wednesday I finally got my opportunity to curl up in the window seat of my father's office. A floppy tattered copy of *The Great Gatsby* lay haphazardly across my knees while I nursed a large cup of tea between my hands.

The door creaked open, and the smiling face of Rowen popped through the space. "Can I come in?"

"By all means, make yourself at home," I grumbled, eyes going back to the fantastic party being depicted on the yellowing pages.

"Claire," Rowen warned. I sighed once and turned my attention to her hovering figure. "Asher informed Xander and me about who you appeared at school with on Monday."

I quirked an eyebrow. "This sounds a lot like a conversation a mother has with her daughter when she hates her new boyfriend."

Rowen laughed lightly, taking up the seat on the other side of me. "No. I just want to make sure you understand who you are dealing with."

"Why does everyone have such a rift about him? He told me already about being an old friend of Lucifer's. It doesn't matter to me, Rowen," I said, standing to set the cup down on my father's desk. We were silent for a while, my back turned to her, waiting for her to fill the silence. I rolled my shoulders back, cranning my neck to watch her. "Gabe is not what everyone says he is. In fact, he is the only one who doesn't treat me like a child they can use for their own gain."

Rowen flinched at my words. I hadn't meant to hurt her, but it was the truth. Xander was toying with me like a puppet on a string that was disposable after it had done its purpose. A hot angry tear rolled down my face. I furiously wiped at it.

"He is dangerous," Rowen whispered, hands

wringing together as if that was the only thing keeping her composed in that moment.

"We are all dangerous in some capacity, Row. It just depends on how we act on those impulses that makes us monsters," I murmured. She held my gaze, hers void of emotion. "If that is all you wanted to speak to me about, you can leave. I have a book to get back to."

I turned away from her, fingertips gripping the underside of the desk to steady myself as the anger pulsed through me. Rowen stepped to leave but paused as she reached for the door handle.

"Do you know why I continue to choose Xander even through all of the madness?" Rowen's voice was deadly calm. "It is because he is the other half to my soul, and not in some romance novel type of way. He quite literally is the other half of my soul that was broken off when we were created. We find out who it is in a ceremony when the council deems it our time."

"Why are you telling me this?" I asked, voice shaking as the nerves traveled through my body.

"Gabriel had his ceremony, and unfortunately

you were not the person who completed him." Rowen's words were harsh, ripping through me like daggers. She craved to wound me enough to ensure I would not run back into Gabe's arms.

Raising my head, I looked into her burning gaze. "Who?"

"Tabitha Manson." Rowen watched for my reaction, but I willed my face to not show one.

"What happens if he chooses to rebel against what the ceremony says?" I asked, relief flooding through me like rain on a hot summer's day.

"Chooses?" Rowen hissed. She shot forward, hand wrapping its way around my wrist. I yelped in pain as she squeezed tight. "The council has the final say. Do your best to remember that, Claire Halloway. I will not have you destroy this plan we have for some teenage love affair. Are we understood?"

I nodded just to appease her. Rowen smiled the same sweet smile she had given me the first day we met. "Good. I am glad we can come to this agreement."

CHAPTER TEN

The bitter sting of reality filled the emptiness in my house. My father was gone and would be until his work at the church was complete. I placed a fresh pack of frozen peas against my bruising wrist. There was something very wrong with the way Rowen had spoken to me that. She had never held the council over my head like today. In fact, Rowen rarely mentioned them by their name at all. It was always Xander who explained the danger they held. Was it possible that Rowen thought the council were the good guys in all of this?

A thunderous knock rattled my front door. I slipped into the entryway silently and waited for another knock to come. Perhaps whoever it was would just go away when they realized no one was home. Another knock came, this time fiercer than the last. I sighed and wrenched open the door to reveal Gabe's annoyed face.

"I didn't realize you were coming over," I said, voice shaking with an emotion I couldn't pinpoint. His eyes narrowed, examining me with his hawk-like gaze. Gabe stepped over the threshold of the home, his body heat radiating off him and on to me. I staggered back. After what Rowen had revealed, my mind raced with a million questions for him. They were stuck in the base of my throat, making it hard to breathe.

"Are you okay?" Gabe questioned. He reached out to touch me, but I shrank away. Turning, I made my way back to the kitchen. The frozen peas were already creating a puddle of condensation on the counter. I picked them up and placed them against my wrist once again. A hiss slid through my clenched teeth at the contact. Gabe came up behind me. "What did you do now? Trip over air?"

I glared at his smirk. "No. I have more grace than that, you buffoon."

"Let me see," Gabe said softly and took the wrist gingerly in his grasp to assess the damage. I didn't pull away. Instead, I let myself melt under his easy strokes as he ran a finger over the bruising. Gabe's eyes darkened, realization of the marks coming to him. "Who did this?"

His voice darkened with every syllable, jaw popping at the tension in the air. I shrugged once, trying to brush off the injury. If I informed him about what had occurred with Rowen, this was going to fall apart. I couldn't keep what I knew in forever, but a little longer wouldn't hurt either of us. When I refused to respond to him, Gabe sent me a pointed look. "Claire. I won't ask again."

"I know about Tabitha Manson," I whispered. The air around us turned stale as Gabe let my wrist slip through his fingertips. He ran his hand over his jawline as the wheels in his mind began to spin so erratically, I could practically see them.

"Xander told." It wasn't a question. Although he was wrong, I understood why he believed this. Xander had wronged so many people in Idelwood. Whether that was because of his own selfish pleasure of being in control or because he truly believed he was in the right, I could not tell.

I shook my head once. "It was actually Rowen."

"Rowen?" Gabe's eyebrows scrunched together. "What would she tell you about Tabby?"

Tabby.

The nickname felt like a punch to the gut. I turned away from him, tears beginning to brim my eyes. "She was trying to convince me you were dangerous because you are defying the council."

Gabe was silent. I slammed my hands against the countertop, sucking in a harsh breath as a sharp pain shot through my injured hand. "She's a hypocrite. Look at her judging your actions when she has gotten herself into such a deep hole that she had to drag us all under with her."

His heavy breathing behind me froze me in place. "I don't care what she thinks of my actions. They are the least of her concerns right now."

"Why didn't you tell me?" I craned my neck to look up at him. Gabe kept his eyes averted from my own. "Was it because you knew that at some point I would be gone, and you could just use me until then? After that, you could run back to *Tabby*."

"Claire," Gabe warned, spitting out my name with a venom I had never heard him use against me. "You have no idea what you are speaking about."

"Oh, I think I do," I whirled on him, pointing one accusatory finger in his direction. "I think you are destined to be with a girl that isn't me."

"I never accepted the ceremony." Gabe stepped into my point, his chest muscles brushing up against my fingertip. "Tabitha Manson knows where I stand on this."

"And where do you stand?" I screamed finally, releasing all the composure I had built up out into the air. My voice reverberated off the cabinets, causing Gabe to flinch back. Then I closed the gap between us, colliding with Gabe's lips. A deep groan came from the back of his throat, lips hungry against mine. The kiss wasn't soft or sweet; instead I poured my frustrations into it and pressed my body further into his.

He growled against the kiss, strong hands coming under my hips and hoisting me up onto the counter. I wrapped my legs around his, pulling him back to me. Gabe's hands trailed down my figure, taking their time to follow the planes of my body in soft sensual touches. A shiver trailed down my spine. I broke the kiss, letting my head loll backward as his lips traced the front of my throat, landing at the sensitive spot just above my collar bone.

"Why do all of our arguments end in this way?" I asked in a breathy whisper.

Gabe chuckled, the sound reverberating against my skin. "Are you complaining?"

"No." I met his hooded eyes. They flicked up to mine through long lashes. "Just saying we should argue a lot more."

"I will keep that in mind," he said before standing straight. Even with me sitting on the counter, he still towered over me. Gabe grasped a loose curl that had fallen into my eyes, twirling it around in his fingertips. "I assume that means I am forgiven for keeping this from you."

"Gabe, you are such a bright guy, but sometimes I wonder if you landed on your head when you fell from heaven."

His fingers stilled, eyes meeting mine in a playful dance. "Was that your attempt to flirt with me?"

I lightly pushed against his chest. "I don't think I will forgive you now!"

"But how could you not with a face like this," Gabe asked, batting his eyelashes at me. I laughed and buried my head in his chest. I took in this moment of pure and utter bliss that could only be achieved when we were alone. No prying council member eyes or nosy angel friends to ruin the moment.

The sound of glass shattering, followed by the searing pain of something burning the back of my arms, caused me to jerk around. In the middle of the island, a flaming bottle of amber liquid burned bright. I let out a gasp, throwing myself away from the fire and into Gabe's arms. He caught me easily, setting me down beside him, but I still clutched onto his T-shirt.

In black, bold letters someone had painted the words **We're Watching**. I knew it was a warning, one from the faceless council that I never wanted to meet. Gabe detached me from his shirt, rushing around the counter in one fluid motion to extinguish the fire with a cup of water from the sink. The linoleum was melted under the bottle, causing the plastic to sizzle into it with a horrid hiss.

"We need to leave," Gabe said. His voice sounded like we stood in a wind tunnel. I nodded numbly in response. My eyes were still trained on the warning. He placed a hand against my arm, causing me to jump before I allowed him to lead me out of the house and into the chill night air.

"I think it is time to call Xander," I whispered. Even in the moonlit night I could see the scowl plastered across Gabe's face. "The council knows, and if they know about me, there is a chance they know about the baby."

Gabe didn't respond but simply reached into his pocket and flipped open his device. He pressed the phone to his ear before stepping away from me to speak to the fallen angel on the line. I could only hear a mumbled version of what was said. Gabe's face was void of emotion as he tried to keep his feelings from spilling over. As much as he wanted to protect me, he understood this was the best move I could make.

Flipping the phone shut, Gabe made his way over to me. "Xander wants to meet."

Chapter Eleven

On the edge of town, a Greyhound bus came and went once a night. There was a rickety streetlight that swung in the wind and flickered every couple of seconds. It barely lit the space it was intended to, allowing Gabe and me to stay hidden in the shadows of the night waiting for Xander to appear.

A car rolled to a stop in front of us, the headlights off and windows so tinted I couldn't see inside the vehicle. The passenger side window rolled down, revealing Mallory sitting next to Xander. I could make out Delaney sulking in the backseat as well. Gabe laid a single kiss against my hairline before opening the back door for me. I slid silently into the warmth of the vehicle.

"I'll look after her, Gabe," Delaney said firmly. They held an intense stare for a moment, seeming to have a silent conversation before Gabe nodded once.

"Are you not coming with?" I asked, mind filling with dread at the idea of being separated at this moment. My eyes tracked his movements as he gathered the seatbelt and clicked it into place across my body. Normally I would argue against it, but I didn't have it in me to debate the action.

"If you both disappear from town tonight, the council will be tipped off that something has occurred." Xander's voice came from the front seat. I kept my eyes trained on Gabe. He sent me a sad smile.

"I will see you soon, love," Gabe whispered, tweaking my chin, and kissing my forehead once again before he closed the door. The car peeled away, and emptiness in my heart like I'd never had before settled in my chest. My entire world had been flipped on its axis, and the one person holding me onto its surface was standing on the other side of the world.

The car ride was quiet. I watched the trees fly by as involuntary tears streaked down my face. I always knew that one day love would break me, but for some reason I never realized that it would rock me to my very core. The trailer came into view, only illuminated by the car's headlights. Asher was leaning over the railing, a cigarette burning at the end of his fingertips. He watched the trees sway just ahead. I stepped from the car, following closely behind Mallory as we made our way up the rickety metal stairs.

"Warned you that this was going to happen, didn't I, Clairebear?" Asher mocked me as I passed. He took one last drag of the cigarette before throwing it on the ground and stomping out the light. I glared at him through my tears, but it didn't seem to faze Asher. He held his hands out toward the door. "After you."

"Knock it off, Asher," Delaney hissed, rolling her eyes, and pushing herself through the group of us to get into the trailer. I followed after her as she led me to the small kitchen. All of us were crammed into it, taking up every inch of space.

"Why do we insist on doing our scheming in here when there is a perfectly good living room just five steps away?" Asher asked, placing himself between the corner of the fridge and the trailer's wall.

Mallory shoved her shoulder into his as she stood in the corner opposite of him. "Because there are snacks in here. All good schemes begin with snacks, Asher."

"Enough," Xander's voice sounded through the confined space. We all turned toward him, waiting for him to continue. "It is obvious that the council has been informed of Claire's knowledge and plans to watch her closely. From now on, you will be staying here for your own safety. You will keep up the facade of school and any church related activities that your father requires, but you will be accompanied by someone in the group. And there is the matter of distancing yourself from the fling you have with Gabriel Moreno."

"That is not negotiable," I spat out. Rowen stood behind him, shooting me a deadly look. A hand rubbed light circles across her stomach in a nurturing way, but there was a sinister current underneath the movement. I had met that side of her this afternoon. "Gabe and I are none of your concern."

"He was not a part of the original plan. Once Liliana is born, you will need to leave town with her and can never return to Idelwood," Xander said calmly, his eyes watching my every movement.

"Never?" I sucked in a deep breath. "I didn't agree to that. What about my life here?"

"It will cease to exist," Rowen said. "You will need to blend into a new town and stay hidden from the Elite. The medallion will hide you and Liliana until the time is right. But you will always be in hiding, Claire."

Hot beads of sweat gathered at the back of my neck. The small kitchen's walls began to close in on me, swaying back and forth as they went. The tan and orange tiles below my feet muddled together into a brownish color, causing my stomach to twist in disgust. I burst into a sprint from the kitchen, pushing past everyone to get out the front door. I threw myself down the stairs in rushed steps. The contents of my lunch splattered against the grassy area next to the trailer. Wiping my face with the back of my hand, I tried to steady my breathing.

My life in Idelwood was coming to a close, and the deal I had made with the devil would soon be cashed in.

CHAPTER татр TWELVE

The library was empty the next afternoon. With the semester ending for fall break in a couple of weeks, the number of students sticking around for study periods were few and far between. My eyes scanned the book in front of me one last time before I slammed it shut. I couldn't concentrate on the romance in a faraway land when my life was shattering around me.

"Remind me again what that poor book ever did you?" a male's voice teased. I scowled at Gabe who was leaned up against the bookshelf in front of me. The crooked smile he was flashing me made my stomach flutter slightly.

"Nothing." I muttered, "I just can't concentrate

on something so meaningless when my life is teetering on the edge."

Gabe stepped forward to the desk where I was sitting at. His finger traced underneath my chin, angling it up so I would look at him. "We will find a way to get the council to leave you be."

I rolled my eyes. "They are the least of my worries at this point."

"I took you to Xander last night — am I wrong to assume he has a plan?" Gabe sent me a narrowed look. His hand absentmindedly cradled my cheek. I leaned into the touch, watching him closely to see if he would let me in on his thoughts.

"I think I got in over my head, Gabe," I said, words coming out in a soft whimper. His attention snapped back toward me, eyes raging with a fire that was built up from years of hatred.

"What do you mean? Did you agree to help Xander blindly?" Gabe's voice was a deadly calm. I pulled myself out of his touch as if it burned me. Twisting my arms around my body, I could feel the tremors of fear rack through me.

"I thought I was doing the right thing," I choked

out. "Everyone told me it was the right thing to do."

"What is, Claire?"

"I am to take the child to a safe place once she is born, but what Xander forgot to mention was that I can never return to Idelwood." I averted my eyes away as his face dropped. The devastation coating his features was too painful to look at; it made my heart clench in uncomfortable sputters that I wasn't even aware it could do. "Gabe, I am so sorry."

"It's not your fault." Gabe pulled my face back to look at him. Both of his hands rested on either side of my face. I still couldn't meet his eyes as the first tears began to pour down my face. "Hey. Claire, look at me."

After a moment I met his gaze, blue eyes shining with determination as he said, "We are going to fix this. If it takes my last breath, I will make sure you are safe from all of this madness."

Xander stood in a clearing, looking angelic in the golden light of the fading sun. The irony of the whole image seemed laughable. I gripped down tightly on Gabe's hand. He pulled me closer to him, and my nose brushed up against the side of his arm. The wind picked up, sending his intoxicating scent swirling around me and taking the edge off my nerves.

Xander kept his back facing us. "You always had a way of tangling yourself in the nefarious plans of another. Now, I see you have wormed your way into mine."

A guttural growl came from Gabe as he glared at the fallen angel. "I am trying to worm my way *out* of it, but you have your claws so deep in this town that it is impossible to avoid. What I can't comprehend is why bring Claire into this?"

"Better claws than false venom," Xander craned his neck to the side to look at me over his shoulder. "And Claire, well, that would be a question that would have to be answered by Rowen, who is unfortunately preoccupied at the moment."

"She is not a pawn in this vengeance you want against the council, Xander," Gabe spat at him. Xander only chuckled at the accusation. I could practically feel the heat steaming off Gabe as Xander turned to finally face us. "What is it going to take?"

"Claire cannot run from this." Xander crossed his arms over his chest, eyes trained on me. I shrank back from his stare. It was cold and emotionless. Xander did not care about my wellbeing—he only had one goal.

"There has to be another way," Gabe pleaded with the fallen angel. The emotions shaking his voice made me want to sink into him, but I resisted the urge. "Anything, I will do anything.""

Xander shook his head. "No, the medallion chose her, and it won't release its hold on her until it believes Liliana needs it. You, out of all of us should know the consequences of trying to reverse that decision."

I reached up and toyed with the object hanging between my breasts. Most days I forgot it was there. Now, it felt like a boulder hanging from the chain. The weight was suffocating, pulling my body into its power. I gulped down a few deep breaths, trying to ignore the nagging pull of the medallion.

"And there is also the council to consider." Xander flicked a speck of dirt off his black shirt. His eyes met mine once more, and I could see where the stories of a monster hidden inside him stemmed from. Pitch-black orbs watched me with villainous intent. "They would bury you under the rubble of this town if it meant keeping what lurks in the shadows hidden."

Chapter Thirteen

A soft glow of the setting sun shone down on the dashboard of Gabe's truck as it pulled into the gravel path in front of the trailer. I had divided my time between here and Gabe's home. My father was too busy preparing for the upcoming seasons events to be bothered with my coming or going. But there was a gnawing feeling that he was more aware of what occurred in this town and decided to stay out of the crossfire.

The light touch of Gabe's hand brushed against my cheekbone. I turned into his palm, looking up at him. His lips were pulled up in a soft smile, but it did not reach his sad eyes.

"It's only for the weekend," I whispered into

the silence of the truck's cab. My lips brushed a light kiss against his palm that rested on my face.

"Are you trying to convince me or yourself?" Gabe asked. He could read me too well, and that scared me. I sighed, pulling away from him to lay my head back against the seat. "Claire."

The strain in his voice pulled my eyes back to his. The burn of tears threatened to spill over on to my cheeks. Days were ticking down quicker than I could grapple with. I wanted to spend every last second of our scarce time together, but Xander insisted that I was present in the group to keep up to date on the plans. The meetings never went anywhere successful; the voices got loud, and the ideas went in circles as Rowen's due date grew closer.

"There is a fall picnic that the church holds every year," I said, voice cracking. Gabe smirked at me. Of course, he knew about the event. "Why don't we go on a real date instead of hiding in your room?"

"Are you asking me out?" Gabe raised an eyebrow at me. I leaned over and shoved his shoulder lightly. He laughed, gripping onto my arm and pulling me into him, lips hovering inches from mine. I could feel my smile brush up against his as he spoke, "Of course I will take you to the fall picnic. Maybe we can sneak off into a hidden corner of the pumpkin patch and—"

His lips connected with mine, telling me the rest of his idea without words. The arm he wasn't holding onto looped around his neck, and I leaned into him, molding my upper body with his. Gabe released my arm, his hands finding home on the sides of my hips. I took this chance to break the kiss and lift my leg over his to straddle him. Gabe caught my bottom lip with his teeth, causing me to gasp against his lips. I moved closer into the kiss, savoring the taste of him in these stolen moments.

Gabe's mouth moved down to my exposed shoulder, leaving a trail of kisses. Each one was softer than the last and undoing me as I sucked in a sharp breath. Throwing my head back, my eyes fluttered shut. The strap of my dress slipped down leaving more skin exposed for his taking. I needed his lips on mine and everywhere at that same time. Straightening up, I pulled him back to me with a single finger. My hands slid down his shirt before finding home underneath it, fingers tracing the smooth planes of his abdomen. Gabe gripped the back of my head, hand tangled in curls as he pulled me close.

A bang of the trailer door hitting the metal ripped us apart. I whipped around to see Mallory and Asher standing on the deck, watching us with amused looks. Mallory lifted one slender hand to wave at us, a laugh bubbling out of her lips as she did. I turned back into Gabe, my face hot with embarrassment. Leaning down toward the door handle, I opened it before untangling myself from him who followed swiftly after me. The truck's door hid me from the view of Asher and Mallory, but I could still feel their lingering eyes. Pulling at the roots of my hair, I tried to settle the wild strands down.

"I will see you in two days," Gabe muttered. I looked at him, taking a mental picture for my time away and then nodded. He laid a single kiss on my hairline. "Don't let them tease you too much, love."

I rolled my eyes before making my way around the vehicle. The sound of the truck's door slamming and the engine rumbling to life made the sinking feeling in the pit of my stomach rise. I glanced over my shoulder, making eye contact with Gabe once more as he pulled away into the trees.

The sound of arguing pulled me from my dreamless sleep on the couch. For the first time in days, I hadn't had nightmares about monsters coming for me in the dead of night. Aspyn's dark hair flew around the corner before she appeared in the hallway and was out the front door. Mallory was hot on the angel's heels, her soft voice calling after her. None of them acknowledged me, so I just pulled the wool blanket closer to my body as the chill from the open door filtered into the trailer.

Asher's eyes watched mine as he disappeared out the door to where his twin was. I could only hear bits of mumbles as the three of them spoke. Then Mallory was flying back into the kitchen like a bat out of hell. I bolted up, untangled myself from the blankets, and launched myself at her.

"A carnival." Mallory's voice was high pitched with excitement. She bounced on the balls of her feet, waiting for the group in front of her to respond. Xander only raised a questioning brow in her direction. "Aspyn suggested a distraction. What better way than using a fall carnival to keep the locals entertained while the council tries to keep normalcy in Idelwood? It will be the perfect way for Claire to slip out of town without raising any alarms."

The air around me went dry as I sucked in a ragged breath. Mallory turned, finally noticing my presence behind her. Her mouth bobbed open and closed, trying to find the right words to comfort me. I shook my head, turning on my heel and heading out into the night. The wind brushed up against my heated skin, and I savored the feeling as I tried to calm my erratic breathing. My hands gripped the metal railing of the porch. I leaned down, head resting against the cool surface like it was the only thing grounding me to the earth.

"Rough night?" a male's voice teased to my left.

I rotated my head against the metal to see Asher's smirking face. The soft glow of a lit cigarette hung over the railing, dangling in between his pointer and middle fingers. A ghostly smile played against his lips as he caught me staring.

"More like rough year," I grumbled out. Asher raised the cigarette to his lips, inhaling deeply before letting the smoke catch in the wind. I narrowed my gaze at him. "Since when have you taken up smoking? That'll kill you one of these days."

"Claire," Asher laughed, "I am an immortal being. This won't even scrape off the surface of my lifespan."

Standing from my position against the rail, I rolled my eyes at him, shoving a shoulder into his. Asher had been so serious for months, and I'd missed this playful side of him.

"November twelfth." Asher's face lost its joy. "That is when you leave town."

Reality hit me in the gut again, and I felt sick thinking how close that date was. Five days. That was all the time I had left in Idelwood. The only time I had to memorize every moment with Gabe until we met again. By then, he could have moved on with someone like him. Someone like Tabitha Manson.

"At least one of us is getting out of hell," Asher mumbled. I turned to question him, but fury burned into the stare he was shooting into the woods. Watching him for a second longer, I threw my arms around him. The hug was awkward, but it was more about the sentiment I was going for. Asher's body shook with laughter when I pulled away. "Getting sappy on me, Halloway?"

"Never." I flashed him a devious smile. "You know, out of everyone I am going to miss you the most."

"But if Mal asked you who, you would tell her the same thing." Asher eyed me, throwing the cigarette on the ground and stomping it out with his foot. In a couple long, drawn-out strides, he found a seat on the stairs of the porch, patting the spot next to him for me.

Skipping over, I bent at the knee and smirked at him. "Of course. I wouldn't want to hurt her fragile feelings now, would I?"

He shoved me playfully, causing me to topple onto the step in the most ungraceful way ever. My laughter filled the night air as I straightened myself out.

"I'll miss you too, Clairebear," Asher finally said. Turning to look at him, I met his gaze. It was swirling with so many intense emotions. "I will never be able to thank you enough for what you are sacrificing."

I nodded once, taking in his words. All this, everything he was trying to stop, was because of a ceremony that didn't guarantee anything. Liliana could grow to resent the place she would only hear stories about. Stories I would be telling her. Asher had finally broken down a few weeks ago and explained his side. Why he cared so much about everything going smoothly. I opened my mouth to say something, but a movement in the trees caught my attention. The swish of white fabric billowing behind a childlike form as it disappeared into the forest's depths.

Shooting up from my spot, I jumped down

the stairs and sprinted into the middle of the tree line. Asher followed closely behind me, watching as I frantically whipped my head around to find the figure. Whatever had been watching us had seemed to evaporate into thin air.

"Where did it go?" I whispered. Asher looked at me with wild eyes. "You saw that, right? Something was watching us out here."

"Claire." Asher's voice was soft. He had his hands out in front of him as if he were calming a wild animal. I stepped away from his touch.

"I *am* losing my mind, aren't I?" I asked. Breathing was becoming increasingly harder under his concerned gaze. "I swear I'm not crazy, Asher. There was something there."

"I believe you," Asher spoke firmly, his hands landing on the top of my shoulders, steadying me. "Is this the first time you have seen something like this?"

"No," I admitted. "There was another time. It was a young girl, and she was drenched in blood. One second there and the next Gabe was shaking me out of a trance in the middle of a field next to my house."

Asher's eyebrows fused together in confusion. "And you said it wasn't you who spoke to Aspyn?"

"What?" I asked. The gears behind Asher's eyes were turning as he began to think. I started to speak once again, but he held his hand up, cutting off my thought.

"Don't tell anyone about this. Not even Rowen or Xander," Asher said, voice shaking slightly with anger. "Do you understand?"

"Yes," I squeaked out. Turning once again, I looked into the trees where another swish of white fluttered across my vision. The walk back to the trailer felt like I was strolling into the lion's den. And I was now the lion's favorite prey.

Chapter Fourteen

My father didn't say goodbye before he set off to work this morning. Not that he was aware of the fact it was the last time he would see me. I would be only a memory after tonight to him. Maybe in the form of my younger self, when I would dress up in my mother's gowns and run through the hallways of our home. So blissfully unaware of the evils in this world.

The stairway was dark as I descended it and made my way out the front door. My arms were full of fall items for the booths that would soon be set up for the carnival. At the edge of my yard, just past the gate, stood Gabe. His hands were in his pockets, face seething with anger as he watched me approach. I hadn't told him I was going to be leaving town tonight, and the sickening feeling in my gut told me he just found out.

"You weren't going to disappear and not say anything, were you?" Gabe's voice was scarily calm. I pushed through the metal gate, the hinges letting out a ghostly hiss.

I clenched my teeth together, trying to gather the words I had been mulling over for the past five days. It was selfish, but I hadn't wanted to ruin the last days we had together. Sucking in a harsh breath, I said, "I thought it would be easier this way."

"Easier?" Gabe asked, his voice rising slightly.

I ignored it and shouldered past him to start down the street. The items in the box jostled about as I hoisted the weight onto my left arm. Gabe noticed me struggling and took the box out of my hands, ignoring my protest. "You shouldn't have made that decision on your own, Claire."

I stopped mid-step, casting angry tear-filled eyes at him. "This was the one thing I had control of, Gabe. While everything else in my life has been controlled by others, I got to decide whether to tell you I was leaving. And I chose not to for my own selfish desires. For that I am not sorry."

Turning on my heel, I dashed away from him, leaving the cardboard box full of bright fall colors with him. I was not sure it would make it to town square no matter who carried it. Gabe called after me, but I kept running, allowing the hot tears to spill down my face.

When I arrived in the middle of town, Celia thrust another box filled with fake blood and bats into my arms. She pointed me off in the general direction of the haunted maze that the high school's theater department was setting up before racing back into her café to check on the food for the evening. Sighing, I made my way through the booths and rides to where Aspyn Faye stood directing people where she wanted them. I narrowed my gaze at her. She was the mastermind behind this entire plan, and just the sight of her gave me a bitter taste. But I couldn't cause a scene. Not out in the open like this.

"Do you need any help?" I asked as I approached her. Aspyn's bright eyes snapped to me, taking my appearance in once before her hands curled around a pair of streamers. The crunch of the paper rippled through the wind.

The feeling's mutual, I assure you.

She bent at the knee, picking up the unrolled streamers before answering me. "No, I think I'm good here, Claire."

Aspyn's tone was short, and the underlying annoyance at my presence rubbed me the wrong way. I huffed an angry breath before turning toward the rows of corn. My feet only made it a few steps before I spun back around and threw the box of Halloween decorations on the floor. The bottle of fake blood exploded, sending a rain of red across my white shirt. It didn't matter at this point. I would have to get rid of it once I left town.

"You're not the only one who has something to lose, Aspyn," I hissed at her. My words were harsh, and I could feel as they cut through her. Aspyn's eyes widened at my outburst, mouth moving to try and defend herself, but I held up one hand. "Some of us just found what they always knew was out there, and it threatens to be destroyed."

The words caught in the back of my throat and came out in a choked gasp. Aspyn stared at me with astonishment. "Claire, don't think I don't know you are risking everything to help them. You are going to lose your home, your fath—"

Angry laughter bubbled out of my chest. "My father? I couldn't care less about him. And I was never in love with this town."

Idelwood had never been home—until I discovered Gabe was chained to it. But even if I stayed, I could not have him. Not with the council watching every move I made and taking into account any slip ups that could be my last.

Aspyn shook her head. "Then what else could be left here? We will still be around, I promise that."

She didn't know. None of the group had told her about my relationship with Gabe. Maybe they thought she was the rat in the group, but if that were the case, why allow her to plan this grand escape for me? Furrowing my brow, I waited for it to click in her mind, but movement behind her head caught my eyes. Gabe stood arms crossed over his chest as he watched me spit fire at Aspyn. Her fingers laced with mine, and I ripped away from the touch like it had burned me.

I kept my eyes trained on Gabe as I spoke again, "Just be grateful you have Finley. Some of us aren't so lucky to be in love with a person we can spend the rest of our mortal lives with."

Turning on my heel, I reached down and retrieved the blood-covered cardboard box before stepping into the twisted maze of horrors.

Chapter Fifteen

The night air was thick with screams and the stench of cornstarch blood. I concentrated on staying hidden between the cornstalks that had been delicately hammered into the ground. It had taken the student council three days to get each piece placed perfectly. A huge waste of time in the grand scheme of things, but the poor souls of this town didn't know that.

A shriek of terror ripped through the maze as a group of teenage girls passed by a scare actor a few feet in front of me. I flipped open my phone, the light illuminating the pages clipped together in a messy heap. I was in charge of making sure everything went smoothly and no helpless kid truly got stuck in the maze. Asher's name appeared across the caller ID, and I knew there was only one reason he could be calling me.

"Asher?" I questioned, placing the phone flush against my ear. There was a choked gasp followed by unintelligible whispers from the other line. "If this is some kind of sick prank, I am really not in the mood for it."

"Claire, you need to get to the church immediately." Asher's voice finally came through the line. It held a sternness that only my father had ever given me. I turned on my heel, heading through the twists of the corn. "I can't speak much longer, just confirm you are on your way to us."

"I am coming now," I said, voice at a hushed whisper. "Asher?"

There was another pained groan in the background of the call. Asher mumbled something before responding to me. "Everything is going to be okay."

He must have heard the fear in my voice, but those simple words washed a sense of calm over me. The line cut off, leaving me in the silence of the night. I paused for a moment, scrolling through the contacts on my phone for Gabe's number. I needed to see his face one last time. To have him wrap his arms around me and tell me we would meet again. Even if it was a lie, I would cling to that as if it was my lifeline. I dialed the number, the phone shaking as I held it to my ear. It went to voice mail, the long beep signaling that I could leave a message.

"Hi," I breathed out. "Look, I am headed to the church, and I need to see you. I'm sorry for everything I said today. It wasn't my best moment to say the least." Tears began to build in my eyes as my voice shook slightly. "Gabe, if you don't get this message in time, I just want you to know I love you. And not in a this-is-my-last-chance-to-tell-you sort of way. I love you with every fiber of my mortal being, and I have known for a while. We will meet again. I might look a little different but know that my heart will always be yours. Until my final breath."

The voicemail cut me off, informing me that if I wanted to rerecord to press the pound sign. Ending the call with a shaky hand, I let out a muffled sob. My chest heaved up and down in painful breaths. Letting out a long, exasperated scream, I hurled the phone into the darkness. I stared at the light as it faded into the pitch-black night. Turning on my heel, I raced through the corn. A side exit would lead me directly to the church. It was a focal point of the Idelwood, and the locals knew how to easily get back to town if they stumbled upon it. Busting through the exit, the church was almost completely dark, except for a single light just barely illuminating the sanctuary.

"Claire?" Rowen's musical voice rang out over the wind that had begun to pick up. I turned toward the side of the church. Rowen stood shaking against the cold in only a light cream nightgown. She looked at me, but it was almost as if she was staring directly through me.

"Row, you shouldn't be out here." I rushed forward. She stepped away from me as I tried to grasp her shoulder. I scanned her body. Rowen showed no sign of the pregnancy which had plagued her just hours before. "Where are Xander and Asher?"

"They were never here." Rowen's voice was void of emotions. "It was all a game. Everything is always a game, Claire."

And then she turned, disappearing into the side entrance of the building. I scrambled after her, but when I entered the sanctuary there was no sign of her. In fact, the only sign of life was a child cradled in a small bundle of purple cloth. I approached slowly, the bundle's light gurgling sounds and a whispered lullaby filling the room. My feet bounded to the front pew, and I could finally see Nathaniel Caldwell's face.

He glanced up at me, gaze holding my own before dropping back to the baby. "My dad told me I had to wait here for you."

"Where did he go?" I asked, voice shaking with fear. There was something incredibly wrong with this scene. Rowen had vanished, replaced with a hours-old baby and Nate.

He seemed content, but a darkness washed over his face as he spoke again. "The bad men took him, and she helped."

"Who helped?" I bent at the knee to get eye level with the boy. He shook his head, refusing to give the name of the woman. I sighed looking down at the purple bundle. Light red hair peeked through the fold of the blanket as I brushed it back, trying to get a better look at Liliana. She was beautiful, just as you would expect a child of two ethereal beings would be, and there was a slight glow surrounding her in the dimly lit room. "Can I hold her, Nate?"

Nate eyed me warily but nodded, passing me Liliana slowly. I gathered her up in my arms, and she began to fuss, causing Nate's eyes to grow a size larger.

"Shh," I soothed the newborn, bouncing lightly on my toes to rock her to sleep. Liliana's angry face relaxed as her tiny hand made its way to her mouth. Soft suckling sounds filled the silent church once again.

I looked up at Nate, my mouth opening to ask who had taken his father, but the shattering of glass followed by the heavy stench of smoke filled the church, stopping me in my tracks.

Chapter Sixteen

Thick clouds of smoke billowed from the back of the church. I could barely see in front of me as I gathered Nate's hand in mine, pulling him along as I made my way to my father's office. Liliana began to cry in high-pitched spurts as we reached the door. I shoved my shoulder against the wood, careful not to jostle the baby in my arms. Nate dashed into the smokeless room, blue eyes filling with tears as he looked to me for direction.

"Take your sister into the office and try to climb out the window" I sternly said, handing the newborn to the young boy. Reaching up to the medallion on around my neck I yanked the gold piece from it. The chain snapped with a hiss. I held out the medallion at eye level, watching as letters began to etch themselves into the surface on their own. My gut twisted at the words, and without thinking I turned towards an overturned pew the was covered in flames and threw the jewelry piece at it. The metal hit the surface, cracking down the middle and falling to the ground.

I pivoted back to the children, racing into the room, and slamming the door closed behind me. My hand reached out to stroke the side of Liliana's face, fingers lingering against her cheek for a moment longer. As the doors handle began to rattle, I pointed to a large wooden desk in the middle of the room. "Hide under the desk until I come back, or you think it is safe to go out the window behind you. Nod your head if you understand me, Nathaniel."

He nodded quickly before racing over to the desk. His head disappeared under the wooden surface, and I closed the door tightly behind me. Reaching up to the top of the door frame, I traced the ledge for the spare key we kept up there, but my body was jerked backward.

The air in my lungs was knocked out, leaving me gasping in the middle of the floor. I grappled for anything to defend myself with from the invisible force. My eyes began to water as the smoke filling the church thickened. A sinister chuckle echoed in the darkness as if it were everywhere and nowhere at once. Pushing myself up onto a sideways pew, I planted my feet into the ground and guided myself back to the office door.

Another blow slammed into me, and I could finally see the dark figure of a male. "It is so unfortunate when mortals catch themselves in business that is none of their concern."

I staggered away from the man. My spine meeting a strong grip which restrained both of my hands behind my back. Craning my neck to see my captor, a breathy gasp came out of my lips. "Asher?"

His eyes refused to meet mine, a darkness casting over the normally bright green of them. I shook slightly against his grip, but it only made him dig his fingers into me tighter. The sizzling sound of water extinguishing a flame echo around us.

"Ah, yes. Betrayal is a hard one when it comes from such a tight knit group as yours." The man's voice spoke up once again. I let my eyes travel back to the figure, trying to gather as much of his facial features into my memory before the smoke overtook me again. "Take her to town hall, would you, Asher? I know she is going to be a vital piece of the upcoming trials."

Heavy footsteps traveled further away from where Asher and I stood. My body shook from the shock of what was occurring. Asher released me from his grip, and I spun around to look at him. He held a single finger up to his lips, silencing my words. Stepping back, he bent at the knee and picked up a piece of the medallion before placing it in an unsealed envelope and sticking it under a pile of rubble near the first pew. With a slight head twitch, he motioned for me to follow after him into the harsh night. I sucked the fresh air into my lungs, coughing slightly, as it burned going down.

Asher watched me momentarily before speaking. "I had no choice, Claire. It was either lure you into this trap, or he was going to kill Aspyn."

"You mean rip her wings out?" I spat toward him. He narrowed his eyes at me in warning, but I continued, "So now what? We leave Nate and Liliana in the burning church? You take me to be killed in front of the council for my part in all of this?"

Asher flinched as I slammed my hands against his chest, trying desperately to get him to move from his position. I gasped out a sob, letting the emotions from the past few months bubble out of me. My knees buckled, slamming into the forest floor. Moments later, Asher was eye level with me, removing my hands from their grip in my hair.

"No." Asher's voice was thick with emotion. "You are going to run. Get out of town and leave Liliana's fate to us. Gabe will find you, I promise, but right now you have to get as far away from Idelwood as you can."

"If you don't bring me to the council, you will be—" I grappled for the words. "And the others. What about them?"

"Don't worry about any of us, Claire," Asher

snapped. He hoisted me back onto my feet. "Just go."

His hands pushed me along as my feet found themselves running into the dark forest. I knew the ways out of town from the church like the back of my hand — luckily, because my mind had not yet caught up to my body's movements.

"CLAIRE!" Rowen's voice screamed through the trees. I screeched to a halt, my body flying forward into the cold floor.

Groaning, I listened for another sign my ears weren't playing tricks on me. Silence followed. Not even the rustle of the wind through the tree leaves, which were swaying in the breeze, could be heard. The soft breath emitting from my lips could be seen as the temperature dropped rapidly. I braced my hands against the mossy surface, wincing slightly as I leaned against my right wrist. It was definitely sprained in my tumble. Pain shot through my arm in a pulsing motion as I got to my feet. They grounded themselves back underneath me as another helpless cry shattered the deafening silence.

"CLAIRE!" Rowen's voice was desperate. I spun around, looking to where she could be. A whisp of red flashed through the tree line to my left. I raced toward it, hoping she would stop for a breath.

"Rowen? Are you hurt?" I screamed into the night air. My voice was answered by an earsplitting scream. I clamped both hands over my ears, trying to block out the sound, but this only made it feel like the scream was amplified by the pressure. Grunting from the pain, I continued waiting to catch another sighting of my friend.

"I am by the bridge, near the church. Please hurry, Claire!" Rowen called out, her voice shaking with what could only be fear for her life. I turned again and headed back to the church, my gaze landing on a bright red ribbon tied to a tree. It waved furiously against the wind like blood streaming through the air around me. As I picked up my pace, more red ribbons appeared on the trees. They melded together around me, and as I burst through the tree line, it was as if my vision was covered in a red film.

"Row?" I called out quietly. There were two figures huddled in front of the church's door, giving the perfect view of the building. A small giggle spouted out from beside me sending a chill down my spine. I turned slowly to the sound, coming face to face with Rowen. She was in a long black dress which was cut down the front in a dramatic vee. It was embellished with small red stones that glittered in the moonlight, giving her an otherworldly glow. "Rowen, are you okay? I thought—"

She shook her head at me as if I was just a stupid girl who couldn't catch on to her jokes. I had expected her to reach over and pat my head in the way adults do when they think what you are saying is adorable.

"Claire, Claire, Claire. Did you truly believe Xander, and his gang of misfits had the advantage in this?" Rowen asked, the corners of her lips quirking up in a sinister grin. The other half of the medallion danced in the moonlight as she toyed with it between her fingers. She clicked her tongue at me, jutting out her bottom lip in a taunting motion. "Who do you think has been the one manipulating this entire situation? I have. Who do you think has been toying with your mind? It is weak, just like a mouse against a snake."

I stepped back from her, horror flooding the pit of my stomach as she spoke. Rowen reached out, yanking me back by the arm closer to her. She was strong, nails drawing blood as she gripped down into my flesh. I let out a hiss, pain radiating through me as she began to drag me along. Digging my heels into the ground, I thrashed against her strength.

Rowen whipped around, nose brushing against mine. I could feel her angry breath coat my cheeks. "I think it is time someone teaches the preacher's daughter some respect."

A jolt of pain shot through me, and as the darkness overcame my body, I could see caramel colored eyes glittering with a devilish charm staring back at me.

Chapter Seventeen

When the fog finally cleared my brain, everything hurt. I coughed slightly, sending an excruciating pain radiating through my ribs. Peeling open my eyes, I found myself lying in a concrete cell with just enough room for me to reach out and touch each wall with my arms extended. The door swung open, blasting a bright light into my eyes. I squinted at the doorway for a moment before my eyes adjusted to the head of the council, Abel, staring down at me.

"Mortals are such fragile things." Abel eyed my injuries. "Sometimes we forget the torture we inflict should be dialed back for them."

I glared up at him, waiting for the man to get

to the point of his visit. If he was going to kill me, I assumed he would have already initiated the order. No, he wanted something from me.

"Bring her to the trial room," Abel instructed two guards behind him before turning on his heel and striding out of sight. The two men gripped underneath my arms, and the pain in my body grew to an unbearable rate. I let my head loll to the side, begging for the darkness to return once again. My vision wavered as I was dragged to a dark room and thrown in the middle. My landing was cushioned by something soft, and I allowed my hand to curl around the surface.

Taking in a labored breath, I peered through my eyelashes at what was beneath me. A horrified scream rippled through me. I was lying in a bed of feathers, each one covered in a dark red substance I could only imagine was blood. I pushed myself away from them, but every part of the room's floor held some remnants of the act.

These were their wings. *Asher's, Aspyn's, Delaney's.* I choked on the thought of Gabe's wings being underneath me. There was a dark laugh to my right. I looked up at the sound, catching the wicked stare of Rowen. My pain dissipated from my body in that moment as I launched myself toward her. She sidestepped my attack as one of the guards from before restrained me.

"That is quite enough, Ms. Halloway," Abel's voice commanded from the front of the room. He sat with eleven other men at a long table. Each one glared down at me with such hatred it was a wonder I was still alive.

"Was this your grand plan? Rip out every one of your friends' wings and then kill me?" I asked, my voice coming in a hysterical scream.

Abel scoffed and adjusted the glasses sitting at the end of his nose. "Yes and no, my dear. Ripping the wings out of those rebels was inevitable. The council knew this, but we have no intention of killing you."

"Well, not in the permanent way that is," Rowen's voice called out. I didn't have the energy to meet her gaze.

"Bring it in." Abel motioned toward the door. A small woman entered. Her head lowered as she approached the council with a serving tray. I would have been able to spot this woman anywhere. Even in all black, the café she owned still stuck to her in white flour patches on her sleeves. The tray was covered with a frosted crystal lid. Celia lifted it, revealing a gold chalice with intricate Latin dialect etched into it. As the preacher's daughter, I knew the significance of this piece immediately.

The Holy Grail. Its surface shone in the light, causing the gold of the cup to become translucent. I sucked in a breath, the power of this piece surrounding me like the medallion once had.

"Thank you, Celia. We will summon you once we have concluded our work with the grail." Abel reached out, gripping the ancient piece in his palms. The woman nodded slowly and turned to exit the room. Sad eyes caught mine before Celia disappeared out of sight. Abel was admiring the cup as one of the other council men stood with a bottle of murky liquid in his hands. The man poured a fair amount into the chalice. Abel met my eyes. "You will be drinking from the Holy Grail, my dear. It will give you eternal life, but at a cost."

"And what is that?" I asked, voice wavering with each word.

"You will be Death, my dear. And you will be feared for it."

I could still feel the burn of the liquid traveling down my throat a month later. The chill of the winter air traveled through the empty graveyard, causing me to pull my jacket tighter to my body. My funeral had been a quiet one. The story of the preacher's daughter who had hung herself in the church spread like wildfire. It brought shame to my father's reputation as well. He moved from Idelwood days after the service. Rowen's way of manipulating images allowed the lie to stick.

In moments that I could sneak away, I liked to come visit my final "resting" place. Not to stare at the bland gravestone that had been shoved into the dirt. It told nobody who I truly was. On occasions such as this one a blue-eyed fallen angel would visit.

Gabe stood staring stoically at my grave. I was hidden away from his view in the trees surrounding us. One hand reached out gently; he ran it down the stone before speaking. "I will never forgive myself for this, Claire. You should have had more in life and should never have gotten caught up in our world."

I placed a shaky hand against my lips to muffle the sob caught between my teeth. Gabe looked up, fresh tears glistening against his eyelashes. It took everything in me not to rush out and embrace him. To take all the pain away and run away from this place. But Abel had a hold on me that I could not risk breaking.

Gabe placed a single kiss on the headstone before straightening back up. A choked gasp escaped my lips, just loud enough for him to hear. Gabe whipped around toward the trees, his eyes searching for the source of the sound.

I stilled, bringing forth a darkness around my body to hide me from his prying gaze. Gabe shook his head slightly, mumbling something I couldn't make out before turning and walking down the hill toward town.

He had fallen in love with Death without a

second thought. And I could never reach him again without destroying us both.

EPILOGUE

Idlewood's residents were dressed in their best formal attire tonight. Each person was adorned with a mask upon their face, not knowing what hid behind the glamour of the night. I was in a simple deep-blue dress, my hair tied up in a matching ribbon to keep it out of my face. I looked down upon Rowen as she destroyed her chance of ever gaining Liliana's trust. My summons had come from her when she decided Death was to make a guest appearance tonight, but she was the one who had inflicted it upon poor Mallory Manson.

Chaos rained down on the party as Rowen snaked herself back into the protection of the council's arms. I watched Asher usher Liliana into the trees lining the woods and made my move to follow him. As I slipped through the light, I felt eyes burning on my skin. My gaze traveled to meet Gabe's searing one, which was mixed with anger and astonishment. A look you would give if you were staring at the town's famed ghost. A crash from inside caught his attention, allowing me to draw the shadows around me and follow the trail Asher had left.

Liliana was rushing into the tress as I pulled the darkness away from me. Her emerald-green dress flowed behind her as she ran.

"The rumors are true, then." Asher did not turn to look at me. "Ghosts are real in this town."

"Hello to you as well, Asher," I said softly. He turned to me, taking his time to stare at Death in the face. "I am not here for what you think."

"You mean you aren't here to kill me?" Asher smirked at me.

I laughed, shaking my head at the fallen angel. "No. I am not here to do that."

"You look good, Clairebear," Asher said, motioning toward me in a nonchalant gesture. "I mean, all things considered."

"All things considered?" I said, lips quirking up at the corners. "I think I look pretty damn good for being Death herself."

Asher barked out a laugh of his own, eyeing me in a way that I had missed. I sighed before continuing, "I am here to inform you that Xander would like to meet you."

"Xander?" Asher's face dropped. "Xander Caldwell is dead."

"Yes." I nodded at him. "But that doesn't mean you can't meet with him if you know the right person."

"Does this help come with a price?" Asher moved closer. Eyes intense with even more questions than he was willing to ask.

"No. I just want to help you all again." I smiled sadly. "It will be like old times. I never thought I would admit to myself that I missed you all as much as I have."

"So where does the Queen of Death usually conduct her formal meetings?"

"Why, the Gates of Hell, of course."

IDELWOOD IS FULL OF SINNERS HOLDING BROKEN HALOS AND WICKED SMILES, SWEETHEART.

THANKS FOR READING!

PLEASE ADD A REVIEW ON AMAZON OR GOODREADS AND LET ME KNOW WHAT YOU THOUGHT!

AMAZON AND GOODREADS REVIEWS ARE EXTREMELY HELPFUL FOR AUTHORS. THANK YOU FOR TAKING THE TIME TO SUPPORT ME AND MY WORK! DON'T FORGET TO SHARE YOUR REVIEW ON SOCIAL MEDIA WITH THE HASHTAG **#DARKSACRIFICES** SO I CAN FIND IT AND OTHERS CAN READ THIS STORY TOO!

Acknowledgments

Every reader has that one book that startedit all. For me, it was a book and a person combined that launched me back into my love of reading. After coming home from a movie, I was asked to get the mail by my mom, and I was pleasantly surprised to see she had a package with the return address name E. Cullen written at the top. Inside that package was a copy of Twilight, and I caught my reading itch once again. My mom's best friend since middle school was named Stephanie, and she created magic no matter where you were. From having a waiter send a gift directly from Edward Cullen himself at dinner to creating a beautiful piece of art, she made every second spent with her special. I will never be able to thank her enough for her part in setting me on this path of being an author.

Mom and Dad, words don't suffice when I think of how to thank you. From encouraging words to creating a dress for an author event, you are always there to support and push me to be the best I can be. Thank you for everything you do.

Elijah Selinsky, your support for my writing means more than you know. I hope you know I am never letting you go and dragging you to every book event I attend. Thank you for reminding me the eye color of my characters and dealing with my at least twice-a-day freakouts. I am so glad the universe placed you in my life!

Kales Hickey, oh darling Kales, thank you for being such a light in our chaos trio. From the hilarious memes you send to having the best reactions to books on voice chat, I am eternally grateful for you! Thank you for always encouraging me even when I allowed others to make me feel like I did not belong. Now I just need to get the strawberry scene book in my hands.

And thank you to all the readers who have fallen in love with my characters. I would be nothing without you guys! You are the heart of this story, and I hope you loved book two as much as I loved writing it for you!

Allison Aldridge is an Arizona native who currently resides in Georgia. With a love for all things that have to do with storytelling, she continues to be an active member of the online book community. When she is not writing, you can find her watching hockey with her family or talking about her newfound fictional crush that has appeared in her life on her social media accounts. Allison graduated from Arizona State University with a Bachelor's in English with a concentration in Literature.

CONNECT WITH ALLISON ON:
Website: www.allisonaldridge.com
Instagram: @authorallisonaldridge
Twitter: Alli_Nichole96
Tik Tok: AuthorAllisonAldridge
YouTube: www. youtube.com/allisonaldridge